THE CONSTABLE

and

THE MINER

JOHN P. F. LYNCH

Published by John P F Lynch

Copyright © John P F Lynch 2019

Lynch, John P F
The Constable and the Miner

ISBN 978-0-9923002-6-5 (pbk)

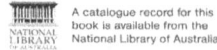 A catalogue record for this book is available from the National Library of Australia

The Author of this book accepts all responsibility for the contents and absolves any other person or persons involved in its production from any responsibility or liability where the contents are concerned.

All rights reserved. No part of this publication may be reproduced, stored in a retrieval system, or transmitted, in any form, by any means, electronic, mechanical, photocopying, recording or otherwise, without prior permission from the author.

Typeset in Bookman Old Style 12 pt

Produced by **TB Books**
P.O. Box 8138
Seymour South Victoria 3660 Australia
Email: info@tbbooks.com.au

Cover Design by Newspaper House, Kilmore Victoria Australia
Cover Picture Front from State Library of Victoria
 "The License Inspected" by S. T. Gill 1869
Cover Picture Back from State Library of Victoria
 "Cobb & Co Coach Scene" by A. Esam 1892

DEDICATION

To my maternal great-great-grandparents – the Hall's, the Symons's, the Cooney's and my great-grandparents – the Keogh's. These four families settled in the Green Hill and Black Hill areas in the Kyneton district between 1849 and 1855. They were true pioneer farmers during the early days of settlement in the Colony of Victoria.

Contents

FOREWORD vii

INTRODUCTION ix

CHAPTER ONE
    The London Bobby. 11
CHAPTER TWO
    To the Colonies 16
CHAPTER THREE
    New Horizons. 25
CHAPTER FOUR
    Lucks A Fortune 50
CHAPTER FIVE
    A New Life 65
CHAPTER SIX
    The Gold Adventure. 83
CHAPTER SEVEN
    Bush Bound 93
CHAPTER EIGHT
    Woodlea. 114
CHAPTER NINE
    Challenges. 124
CHAPTER TEN
    The Pick Pockets 135
CHAPTER ELEVEN
    Achievers All 145
CHAPTER TWELVE
    The Wedding 161
CHAPTER THIRTEEN
    Mystery Solved 169

CHAPTER FOURTEEN
    Promotions All Round 172
CHAPTER FIFTEEN
    A Murder. 176

DEFINITIONS 184

NOTES 189

AUTHOR'S PROFILE. 191

BOOKS WRITTEN 193

FOREWORD

Sometimes people of my generation feel very old, but perhaps it is really that we have seen so much change and development during our stay on earth.

Our days in secondary school were immediately after the Second World War. We had telephones which hung on the wall, pictures that were in black and white only, and there was no television. Lounge room entertainment was either talking with other people, or listening to a radio. At that time the principal history subjects at school were British History and European History.

Hasn't life changed!

One of the changes in education has been the development of the attractive and interesting subject of Australian History – not just as a mundane school subject but as an appealing and arresting form of easy reading historical novel. These volumes are not merely boring books of facts, but an appealing mix of human interest laced with historical settings.

Several earlier such novels were written by authors from overseas. A widely read novel about the uprising on the Ballarat goldfields was penned by an Italian, whilst another very popular author was a South African writing fascinating tales in historical Australian settings.

Now we have come of age and have a plethora of Australian authors writing gripping novels based in Australian settings. Among the leaders is author John Lynch. Some of these authors have a team of researchers doing the background development work, but John does it all himself. He has travelled widely, worked in a variety of places and environments, read widely and made a point of talking with a multitude of people of diverse backgrounds.

The Constable and the Miner reflects the research of the author. It is a gripping but simple tale. The story touches on a great many facets of early Australian life, and encourages the reader to delve further into our national historical background. I am sure you will enjoy the read.

Alan Norman
B. Comm., Dip. Ed., T.P.T.C

INTRODUCTION

The Port Phillip District was founded in 1835 and was still in its infancy in 1851 when it became the Colony of Victoria and separated from the Colony of New South Wales. Early pioneers from Tasmania and overseas gradually moved inland from Melbourne and down from New South Wales with their stock and were soon opening up new land. Then gold was discovered. This event created dramatic and diverse changes in the social, political and financial progress of the new Colony.

The 'gold fever' caused a mass migration of people from Melbourne and the countryside to the goldfields. Shopkeepers, farm hands, tradesmen, police, bank clerks, all walks of life went seeking their fortunes. Some succeeded – most failed. Crime became a major issue, food was costly and sometimes scarce, with many businesses floundering or failing.

This historical novel gives an insight into the lives of two Colonial immigrants – an ex-London policeman and a miner from Northern England, and how law and order was a major problem in those formative years.

Several of these stories are true or reflect those times and have interlinking scenarios to help complete an interesting and exciting historical novel. I trust that this book will be a welcome addition to your library on Australian Colonial History.

John P F Lynch
OAM KSJ JP

CHAPTER ONE

The London Bobby

The fog had been hovering over London for several days. The nights were worse. The dingy gas lights in the streets and alley ways were almost invisible in the murky mist. The good citizens remained indoors; only the criminal element and shady characters would venture into the night to do their mischief. The only sounds were those of heavy boots echoing from the surrounding walls of the alley.

Then out of the mist appeared a male figure. He was tall and strongly built with a distinctive high top hat. A long blue cloak with a small shoulder cape completed his official appearance. He was a 'peeler' or 'bobby' – a London police constable.

He was returning to the police barracks after completing his shift patrolling the East End district of the city. Tonight had been quiet. Most taverns closed early when the fog rolled in and there were only a few ships at the wharfs. Poverty and grog were major problems here, causing violence not only on the streets, but also in people's homes. Not all shifts were this quiet, though. In the past, he had been tested several times with his only support a truncheon and a wooden rattle which was used to summon help from any other bobby within hearing range.

The London Metropolitan Police Force was established in 1829 by Sir Robert Peel and Jeremy Bentham. It was the first apolitical professional police force in the world, charged with maintaining good social order and the protection of the community. Each policeman was issued with an identification number and a distinctive blue uniform. He soon became respected as an essential member of the general community.

John Williams joined the Metropolitan Police Force when he was thirty years of age. He had previously been a stone mason and an occasional prize fighter. When he married, his wife had persuaded him to retire from prize fighting. He had joined the police force so that he could remain close to home. His stone mason job had required him to travel all over London and he was away for days at a time. John was educated by his mother when she was in service with the Duchess of Leeds. During his education, his mother insisted that he speak correctly, with a cultured accent.

Consequently his fellow constables gave him the name of The Toff. Even some of the villains knew him by this name.

He was based within a mile of his home, and walked to work in all weather and with the extra strolling on his shifts kept fit and healthy. He was soon promoted to a Senior Constable position; his education and his speech had no doubt impressed his senior officers. He married his childhood sweetheart who had lived at a nearby farm and they soon had two children. George was the first born and two years later, along came Sarah. He was happy with his lot.

The Metropolitan Police Force had a policy of preventing crime rather than catching criminals. It was a good policy but that didn't stop crime. John had had some anxious moments. As he was normally patrolling by himself, he needed to be ever alert and prepared to be aggressive when confronted by more than one villain.

John had once been bailed up in an alleyway by three men. He did not wait for them to attack him, he took the initiative. He pulled out his truncheon and immediately hit the leader hard on his shoulder with it. He felt the collarbone break. He then quickly struck the second villain hard in the ribs, breaking a few of them. The third man grabbed John by his shoulders. John quickly stepped back and rammed his truncheon hard into his stomach. With a whoosh of air from his lungs, the villain collapsed to the ground struggling to breath.

John did not arrest them, he just said to them: "Don't let me see you around here again." He then continued his patrol. He didn't see them again.

Another time, a robbery occurred in the street next to his beat. He heard the 'rattle' from a fellow constable and quickly ran towards the sound. As he ran around a corner, he was confronted by a man running towards him, looking backwards at the other constable.

The running man turned and saw John. He stopped in front of him, and then raised his fist to strike. John stepped to the side and hit him in the jaw with his fist. The man collapsed to the ground as the other constable arrived, panting.

"Good show! You got him. He has just assaulted and robbed the saddler."

John then looked closely at the robber and remarked. "This is the same person that I chased last week after he robbed the tailor."

John tied the robber's hands together, noticing that he had the first two fingers missing from his right hand. He then led him back to the police barracks. He was advised he was a notorious robber who had, up until now, been too quick for the police to apprehend.

His name was Darcy Sykes, a sailor, a well-known thief throughout England. He admitted to committing robberies whenever his ship was in port.

He was charged and ordered to appear at the Old Bailey the next day. John, as his captor, would accompany him with the prison guards.

The next morning John waited outside the cell block and watched as five chained prisoners were loaded into a large black covered-in wagon. John climbed up and sat alongside the driver while two guards sat in seats at the rear of the prisoners' wagon. He was thankful that it was only a short trip to the Old Bailey as the wagon's continual swaying on the cobble stone streets made the ride very uncomfortable.

It was John's first visit to the Old Bailey Court. The building was large and imposing. The main area had ample seating for the many onlookers and several blocked off areas for the judge, the lawyers and the alleged offenders. The small holding cells were below the main floor, which was accessed via a narrow stairway by the prisoners when they were called to appear before the judge.

The trial was fairly quick. John was called to relate the alleged offence. He read from his report, which impressed the judge as very few police presented logical written reports. Some were virtually illiterate. Generally he had to cross-examine the police to obtain the full story of an alleged offence.

The judge only took a few minutes to check the charge sheet information. He looked up and said:

"Darcy Sykes, I find you guilty as charged. You have been sentenced to seven years penal servitude and you are to be transported to the Colony of Van Diemen's Land." Darcy Sykes did not reply.

Sykes looked across at John. "I hope we meet again. I owe you." John shrugged his shoulders and turned away.

Sykes was an orphan who had grown up on the streets of London and in his fifty years had become a notorious thug and robber feared by many of his kind. He was led from the court and later that day taken to Newgate Prison to await transportation to the colony. Within the month he was on his way to Van Diemen's Land.

The judge acknowledged Constable Williams' deed as commendable. "You have performed a worthy deed to make the community safer."

CHAPTER TWO

To the Colonies

John had been in the Metropolitan Police Force for over ten years and had been acting sergeant several times and was destined to be confirmed in the position within the year.

A new police commissioner, an ex-Naval officer, had just been appointed and was seeking to expand the police force throughout England.

John had heard of the plan but he was surprised when he was called into the Commissioner's office and advised, without grace: "I am posting you to Penrith next month. You have been in London too long. Sometime in the north west of England will give you a different perspective. The town will provide you with a single bedroom cottage at a reasonable rent."

John retorted, "I have two children. A single bedroom cottage would not suit me, even if I wanted to go."

The Commissioner looked at him in amazement and then shouted, "Suit you! You're just a London constable. You will do as you are ordered. You will be posted within the month. Dismissed!"

The Constable and the Miner

Jane had been suffering a chest complaint for several months and the local doctor had said that she needed to live in a warmer climate if she ever wanted to improve her health. John had previously approached the Colonial Office about the prospect of a position in the Australian Colonies.

He was advised they urgently wanted immigrants with police experience, in the new Colony of Victoria. They had already recruited several ex-policemen. The attitude of the Commissioner helped John make up his mind.

The day following the Commissioner's edict, John went to the Colonial Office and formally applied for a position in the police force in the Colony of Victoria.

After a brief interview the family was accepted as U.K. Government emigrants. They were advised that the paperwork and travel arrangements would take nearly a month and to keep in touch with them. His family was delighted and they all began to look forward to their prospects of a fresh life in a new country.

John duly received his transfer orders to travel to Penrith. He waited until the day before he was 'ordered to go to Penrith' and then went to the Commissioner's office. He knocked and was called to enter. The Commissioner had two inspectors in his office. John knew one, an Inspector Clifton from an earlier trial in which they had both been involved. They each nodded to him.

The Commissioner said curtly, "Yes, what do you want? My decision stands; you are going to Penrith."

John replied, "I wish to tender my resignation." He paused for several seconds and then said, "sir." The implication was not lost on the two inspectors.

The Commissioner answered, "It's not accepted. Dismissed."

John continued, "I am sailing to the Australian Colonies within the month." He turned to walk out of the office.

Inspector Clifton interjected, "Commissioner, Acting Sergeant Williams is one of our most experienced men. Have you read his file?"

The Commissioner replied, "No, I don't need to read his file. There are plenty of men wanting to become policemen. No one is indispensable."

John turned and walked out.

At the end of his shift that day, Inspector Clifton approached him. "Williams, you can stay as long as you want; you don't have to finish tomorrow. I'll handle the Commissioner."

John thanked him. The extra money would be handy.

John and his family were excited to be leaving London and looked forward to their adventure, although they were saddened to leave their friends. They had been in the area for over ten years and had become part of the community. However, they were kept busy deciding what to take and what to sell. They were all relatively young – John forty-two years, Jane forty years, George twenty years and Sarah eighteen years of age.

They decided to only take essential items and nothing bulky. They reasoned – correctly – that as the settlement in the Colony of Victoria had begun less than ten years ago and was now becoming established, they could either buy or make what they would need when they arrived.

John continued to report for duty. His name was still entered on the daily duty roster, courtesy of Inspector Clifton. He saw the Commissioner around the barracks but nothing was said.

John found out that the Commissioner had had six other resignations from experienced men and questions were being asked in high places as to why this was occurring. His overbearing Navy attitude within the police force was not being accepted by his fellow officers and constables.

The East End London wharfs were occupied by sailing ships from all over the world, with all types of cargo passing through their many warehouses. Two weeks before John was to embark to the Colony of Victoria, a fire erupted in some cargo on the wharves. The flames were fierce and with the direction of the wind, the warehouses were being threatened. The men who were manning the water pumps were directing their hoses into the middle of the cargo on fire and were retarding the progress of the fire.

When all of a sudden a ball of fire exploded and flammable material blew onto the roof of a single fronted three story building, opposite the row of warehouses and started another fire.

John was given the task of evacuating and keeping people away from this risk area, but unbeknown to all, some people were still in this building. They had been watching the fire on the wharf through an upstairs window. John heard the cry of help from behind him. Looking all around, he saw two people at the first story window. The roof of the building was on fire and there was no way the firemen could get water to that height. The building was doomed.

John ran to the front door, pushed it open and ran up the stairs. The interior was very hot and smoke gushed onto the first floor landing. He ran through the smoke and smashed open the locked door by charging it with his shoulder to find two teenage girls, crying and screaming.

He grabbed both of them by their arms and dragged them to the smoke filled landing. One girl panicked and got free from John's hold and ran back into the room. John picked up the other girl and took her down the stairs where another policeman took her from him and carried her out of the building. John then ran back upstairs to the room and bodily carried the other girl to the landing. It was now full of smoke. John felt for the stair rail and felt his way down the stairs, step by step, as the heat became more intense. He burst out into the street coughing violently.

Other policemen dragged him and the girl away from the building where the first floor window now had flames billowing from it. The building was soon completely destroyed. The following day John wrote a report for the Duty Inspector, who had also collected reports from several other witnesses.

Next day the Inspector called John and asked him about the locked door. "Yes, the door was definitely locked." Two days later the Inspector invited him into his office and told him that they had arrested and charged the building owner with 'Conducting a Brothel and Endangering Life' of the girls. He had admitted to locking the girls in the room, as they were 'his prostitutes'.

Unknown to John, Inspector Clifton, as Acting Police Commissioner while the Commissioner was on temporary leave, had recommended him for an Humane Society Bravery Award. A month later, the recommendation for the Award was duly approved by the Humane Society.

The Commissioner was not very impressed when told of John's award. Protocol required that it was his duty to present the award to him. Worse was to come. Someone had told the newspapers of the Penrith incident.

This caused the Commissioner extreme embarrassment, particularly when he was forced to acknowledge to the newspapers reporters that Acting Sergeant John Williams had resigned because of his insistence that 'an experienced policeman had been ordered to relocate against his will'. A week after the court hearing regarding the brothel keeper, John finally resigned from the police force.

On his way from the barracks John visited Inspector Clifton to say goodbye and to thank him for his support.

The Inspector handed him an envelope. "I wrote this recommendation for your future employers when I was Acting Commissioner. It may help to progress your career. I wish you well."

John shook his hand and thanked him gratefully.

John and his family embarked for Melbourne nine days after the brothel owner court hearing.

The ship was a hive of activity. Trunks, bags, animals, and coops cluttered the deck and sailors carried ropes up and down the rigging.

John's family was pleased to get to their quarters. The voyage would take about four months. Even though they were travelling steerage class, they looked forward to their sea adventure. The steerage accommodation was clean, although it was cramped. Most of the other passengers were government assisted, mainly selected farmers and tradesmen seeking a new life for their families. The meals were very basic but wholesome. Very few of them were ill during the voyage although some suffered seasickness when they encountered rough seas.

The SS Sea Spray sailed due south, heading to Cape Town. It would not be stopping at any other ports. The sea was mainly calm with small waves and mild winds.

John and the family sat for hours looking for fish. They often saw flying fish streaking from one wave top to another. Sometimes they saw the sea churn with schools of small fish, birds diving to catch them. An occasional whale would bring everyone up on deck. If it sounded with a water spout it was a bonus for the viewers.

George befriended a young cadet who was being trained by the Captain. Young Will was the son of another ship captain who thought that it would be better for his son to be trained under someone other than himself. Will was happy with this arrangement and duly introduced George to the Captain.

The Captain was a stern looking man and ran his ship accordingly but he was pleasant when he asked George a few questions concerning his family's comfort and destination. He commented that he believed Melbourne would one day be a major world destination. In a very short time it would be.

When Will was off duty, he showed George around the ship. They even climbed the ratlines up to the yardarms, which didn't please George's mother. She wouldn't look up at him! George was shown how to tie the many knots used by the sailors and, with practise, he slowly mastered the art.

His mother and sister, Sarah, had brought books to read and pass the time. Fortunately other families also had books in their possession and after they were read, book exchanging became a popular past time.

John had a circle of friends who sat and swapped stories of their lives. It was surprising the interesting stories people told of their lives and other stories they had heard. What more stories would the Colonies have in store for them?

The stopover in Cape Town was brief. The crew picked up water, fruit, vegetables and some live sheep to replenish the ship's larder.

John and his family went ashore for a few hours. Jane's legs felt wobbly for a short time when she first walked along the wharf. She had been used to anticipating the rolling of the ship's deck. The wobbly feeling soon stopped.

The ship sailed on the next tide heading due east for the Australian Colonies and to the adventure of a new life. Depending on the winds, the voyage would take around another six weeks.

Two weeks out of Cape Town the westerly winds became stronger and the waves were higher with a stinging spray. It was no longer pleasant to go out onto the slippery deck.

John wedged and then tied their baggage to the bunks to avoid injury from them if they moved in heavy seas.

The noise from the waves with the wind roaring and screeching through the rigging, plus the creaking of wooden joints, was eerie. The ship pitched and rolled violently, causing havoc in the galley, breaking plates and food containers. Most passengers just lay in their bunks holding on tightly. Some were praying. A few slept. Most just lay there wrapped in their warmest clothes. The ship had a minimum of sail set as it alternatively climbed a wave and then slid down the other side with a resultant crash, unnerving the passengers.

The fearsome weather was very stressful and some arguments occurred between the passengers over trivial matters.

No one troubled John or his kin. They knew he was a policeman, albeit in waiting until he arrived in Melbourne.

The winds abated overnight and the opposite occurred – mostly no wind. The Captain headed the ship south hoping to find even a breeze. The weather became increasingly colder.

After four days the winds gradually strengthened. The Captain steered the ship north east and then headed east. It was timely, as the cold air was starting to form ice on the wet deck and the rigging. Below decks, the shivering passengers and crew rugged up. The small coal heaters added very little heat.

Over the next week there was a decided improvement in the weather. It was warmer, with strong winds astern. The Captain informed the passengers they should make up for lost time and arrive in Melbourne close to the planned date. The feeling amongst the passengers was now friendly again, much to Jane's pleasure. She had worried for her family's safety during the unhappy period.

The journey now had the passengers anticipating their arrival. The first Victorian coastline they saw had sandy cliffs and inlets backed by green forests. A few farm houses and livestock were visible in areas cleared of trees. They hugged the coast for several days.

CHAPTER THREE

New Horizons

Eventually the ship turned and headed through a break in the coast, with foaming tidal seas carrying it rapidly into Port Phillip Bay. All the passengers were now on deck. The entrance to the bay was narrow and opened into a very wide expanse of water vanishing into the distance. Melbourne was sited north at the top of the bay. When they dropped anchor in Hobson's Bay the ship was invaded by officials, but within a few hours John and his family had disembarked and soon arrived in Melbourne on a barge. Their voyage was over. They were safe and sound in their new country.

On arrival John immediately contacted Police Headquarters. They were expecting him. They quartered him in a small three room weatherboard cottage vacated the week before. He had been lucky. Being married with two children had been to his advantage. It was in Richmond close to the police barracks. The other recruits were unmarried and were sent to the police barracks' living quarters. The cottage was disappointing but they were lucky; many new arrivals were in tent structures. They soon settled into the Colony's chaotic lifestyle.

Although the effects of the Irish famine had decreased over the past few years, the Irish continued being the most numerous immigrants arriving in Victoria. Many thousands had arrived since 1850.

Melbourne was a seething mass of transiting people heading to the goldfields, together with many Melbourne ex-employees.

John found his fellow new recruits to be a very diverse group. He took an immediate dislike to several of them. Their slovenly attitude and general demeanour soon showed on the parade ground. His judgment was correct. The police instructors sent a quarter of them packing within a week.

Their instruction included horse riding, for which John needed some practise. He had ridden in his youth and still remembered the basics.

Horsemanship was essential for travelling, even around Melbourne and its environs, let alone a posting to the vast country districts of Victoria.

He enjoyed the training and had no difficulty with it. Much of the procedural instruction he knew from his time in the London Police Force. Consequently he received a good report from the instructor. After four weeks he had settled into the Victorian Police routine and was now due to be assigned to a district.

Unexpectedly he was called into his Inspector's office. There were three senior uniformed officers in attendance, including the Assistant Commissioner. John was somewhat surprised by their presence but he remained calm. His Inspector walked forward and introduced him to the other officers.

The Assistant Commissioner stepped up and shook his hand. "Welcome, Constable Williams, to our police force. How are you settling in?"

"Fine, sir." John nodded.

After some small talk, the Inspector continued. "We have received a letter from your previous office in London, which contains a Bravery Citation and it is my pleasure to present you with a medal from the Humane Society for 'Bravery in the line of duty'. Congratulations."

John stood motionless for a few seconds and then he managed to gasp out. "Thank you, sir. Thank you." Each of the officers were clapping their hands and smiling – aware of his discomfort.

The Inspector continued. "As you are no doubt aware we have a shortage of experienced police constables. We are also having problems recruiting suitable types, as you know from the group you trained with. So it has also been agreed, that together with your previous experience and your high performance standard since your arrival, you will be promoted to Acting Sergeant. Congratulations again."

John was still enjoying the thrill of receiving the medal and now this!

He was overwhelmed and only said, "Thank you" and shook the offered hands of the other officers.

His Inspector walked him to the door. "Come and see me tomorrow and we will talk more."

John just nodded and left.

He walked to the stables and sat outside in the sun. It was a beautiful day, warm with no wind. He looked at his Bravery Medal – it was a surprise but the promotion as well!

He then read the citation, appreciating that together with the letter of reference, it was part of the reason for his promotion. Inspector Clifton had not only related the incident details but had also commented on Acting Sergeant Williams' initiative and leadership qualities as an example to others.

He mused that his decision to leave the English weather for his wife's health and seek new employment was most fortunate. He had taken a big gamble bringing his family half way around the world to a new country only partly explored, and now they were on the threshold of a new life. He was no longer a 'Junior London bobby'.

When he told his family of his promotion and showed them the medal they were all proud and delighted. They had settled into the cottage even though it was very basic. The main plus thing they enjoyed in their new life, was the weather.

Jane's health was improving in the drier climate and George and Sarah were happy. They were both unsure about future employment and were in no hurry to decide. Together they wandered around town looking at the shops and businesses and along the river. Jane was still taking it easy and resting in the afternoon.

The river was placid with colourful flowering gum trees on its banks; a distraction from the unpleasant view of the hovels on the other shore. They were made from poles and bark slabs with mud filling the gaps and were surrounded by rubbish which mangy dogs scavenged.

John and the other recruits eagerly awaited their postings. He was unsure what to expect and hoped he would be posted to a country town, as he was unimpressed with Melbourne. It was smoky and smelled of garbage and even worse – sewerage was uncontrolled, even polluting the Yarra River which was the prime source of water. Illness was a major source of worry for the Government. In his short time there, John had learnt that this district was the most lawless area in the Colony.

However, it was his fortune, or otherwise, to be posted to the infamous Metropolitan District of

Melbourne. Could it be any worse than the London East End? He would soon find out!

Initially, John spent four weeks with another sergeant who was a veteran of five years in the Melbourne Metropolitan District. He was big man who behaved accordingly. His method to stop a fight was to knock both aggressors to the ground and then walk away.

He treated the drunks in the same way. A quick slap and a boot in the behind sent them on their way. He said it saved paperwork. At the end of the day he enjoyed a drink or two. A couple of times, John joined him at an inn but did not become his regular drinking companion.

The sergeant was a good teacher and John learnt of the local problem areas, criminals' dens and persons of interest. After his four weeks, John took over from the sergeant and had two constables assigned to him.

Jim Lane had served in the British Navy and had been in the force for two years, and seemed a reliable type. The second constable was Len Smith, a Victorian country lad who had only been in the force for six months, strong and friendly. Both were married without children.

The first two weeks were uneventful, only a couple of fights to break up and the nightly collection of drunks who were locked up overnight. His two constables proved their capability and he began to feel comfortable in his role.

John and his constables had just returned from doing their morning rounds and were enjoying a cup of tea, when a constable ran into the Duty Sergeant's office shouting, "The Bank of Australasia is being robbed by an armed gang and they are still inside the bank."

The Duty Sub Inspector heard the shouting and called out, "Get an armed squad together. Any available officer will do."

Within a few minutes a squad of ten armed policemen had assembled and were running towards the bank. John was one of them. He felt the excitement of being involved in an armed bank robbery.

The bank was only two blocks from the police barracks. The building was a single story wooden structure sited on a corner block.

As the squad arrived, a constable ran to the Sub Inspector and pointed to the main entrance. "There are three of them still in there.

"There was a fourth robber who was holding the horses. We were just on a routine patrol and he panicked when he saw us walking towards him and rode off with their horses – that way."

The constable continued. "The two main bank windows are completely painted over with the bank name stencilled, but a side bank window is open slightly. That's where I looked in and saw the bank staff bailed up. I then sent my partner for help. They know that the horses are gone and that they have been seen but they have made no attempt to escape from the bank. I just waited for you."

"Have the robbers made any demands? How many other people are there in the bank?" the Sub Inspector asked.

The constable replied, "No demands have been made and I counted six people, all sitting opposite the window over against the far wall. The robbers were standing near the main door."

"Could you see any other doors?" asked the Sub Inspector.

"Yes, only one," answered the constable. "Opposite the main door is a single steel door."

The Constable and the Miner

A man ran to the Sub Inspector. "I'm the Assistant Manager. Can I help? I have just heard of the attempted robbery. The robbers can't get into the strong room. It has a dual lock and I have the second key."

The Sub Inspector asked, "Is there another entrance?"

"Yes, there is a door in the covered-in alleyway behind the bank. The alleyway has locked iron gates at the entrance. We use that entrance when transferring gold bullion."

"Draw me a diagram of the bank, its walls, windows, doors and the strong room. Williams, come with me and give me your opinion. We need a plan to get into the bank. You're the next senior officer here, so get your thinking cap on quickly," said the Sub Inspector.

The diagram showed the only other entry into the bank was via the alleyway door. This door opened to a passageway between the strong room and the continuation of the wall where the hostages were lined up. The Assistant Manager advised that he had keys to both the iron gates and the rear door.

The three of them walked to the alleyway. The gates were rusty and John suggested that the hinges be doused with oil in case they creaked during opening. This was soon done. They opened the gates cautiously without any noise occurring. So far, so good. They unlocked the rear door, then quietly walked to the inside steel door and oiled its hinges.

They then retreated to the alleyway to discuss a plan to enter the bank, without placing the hostages in danger.

A constable ran up just as they started. "The robbers want to negotiate with you."

The Sub Inspector walked away by himself to think on a realistic plan of action. He returned and told John,

"Get your best man. We won't try to enter through the front door. Innocent people could be wounded."

He paused. "I will distract them by talking with them through the side window while you two open the middle door and subdue the robbers. You must be prepared for a gun fight.

"Hopefully the hostages will remain where they are now and be safe. Williams, you are an experienced officer and I have every confidence in your ability to resolve this situation."

John went to the group of constables and saw Constable Jim Lane. He called him over. "Constable, I want you to accompany me to do an armed arrest of the robbers. You and I will enter the bank through the middle door. The hostages will be on our right and the robbers on our left. The Sub Inspector will be negotiating with them, diverting their attention. Are you with me?"

Jim smiled and just nodded.

John was armed with two six percussion revolvers and Jim had a double barrelled percussion shotgun.

John and Constable Lane entered the passageway with the assistant manager. He inserted his key and turned it slowly. It was noiseless. They all took a deep breath as John slowly pushed the door ajar. It was hinged on the right and John peered through the open door gap. The three robbers were near the side window listening to the Sub Inspector as he talked.

John's heart was racing. He nodded to the constable. The constable returned a thumb's up. John quickly pushed the door fully open and they burst into the bank.

John shouted, "Surrender in the Queen's name."

The constable was first through the door with his shotgun at his shoulder aimed at the nearest robber.

The robber raised his pistol. The constable immediately fired his shotgun. The blast of six shot hit the robber in the chest and, with a stunned look on his face he slowly fell forward – dead. The constable aimed a second time and squeezed the trigger but the shotgun misfired. Fortunately John had already aimed and fired one of his revolvers and hit another robber in the shoulder who spun around and fell to his knees.

His next shot hit the wall alongside the head of the third robber who instantly threw up his arms. "Don't shoot!" The siege was over within thirty seconds and the hostages were safe and sound.

John ran to the window. "It's over. We have them."

Jim opened the main door for the other policemen to enter. The Sub Inspector was delighted to see the robbers apprehended and the hostages unharmed.

The police removed the dead body and arrested the other two offenders. The manager was smiling and shaking hands with everyone. He was happy his customers and his bank were all safe.

John and the constable returned to the barracks and sat quietly together for a few minutes saying nothing.

John eventually spoke. "I must admit that I was very nervous, but you looked calm. Have you been in a situation like this before?"

Constable Lane just smiled again. "Yes, I have. I was a British Marine and have had been in a few confrontations before, but I was still nervous. Being nervous gives you an edge."

John laughed. "Well I picked the right man for the job."

John told his family of the attempted robbery. He wanted them to know the full story before they heard of it from someone else.

Jane often worried about John's safety but she kept it to herself. This time she cried. John comforted her as best he could. She soon settled down.

The children were more circumspect and accepted their father's role in the community.

A few days after the incident a shopkeeper came to the police barracks to report three horses had been left tied up outside his shop for several days. The police inspected the saddle bags and horse brands and it was discovered that they had been stolen from a New South Wales cattle station. The horses had been loaned to some itinerant drovers to join the station's team to muster cattle for the Melbourne market.

The two captured robbers said that they had wasted all their wages on grog and then decided to rob a bank and stow away on a ship. They had not intended to harm anyone. Unfortunately for them the Judge did not agree and they were both hanged.

The sentence upset John.

The week following the bank robbery the Police Department conducted an assessment of the effectiveness of the Sub Inspector's management of the incident. His speedy action and subsequent performance, together with control of the crisis, was judged as excellent. Acting Sergeant Williams and Constable Lane's efforts were both regarded as meritorious. The three were awarded The Police Medal.

The next week John and his team were back patrolling the streets collecting drunks and arresting petty thieves. Sometimes there were other duties. One particular assignment he enjoyed, was escorting the prisoners in the 'Black Maria' wagon to the Pentridge Stockade at Coburg, which was a suburb some twenty miles north of Melbourne.

The wagon trip to Coburg and return to Melbourne

took all day but it was a pleasant trip and they could relax as the prisoners were in chains in the locked wagon with armed warders riding on top.

John preferred to ride about thirty yards behind the wagon. If there was to be trouble, it would be in front of you and was easy to contain. He had learned this strategy in London and had seen it work when some unchained prisoners broke out through the roof of the wagon. They didn't get far. The constables following soon ran them down.

The road to Coburg had small settlements either side. Dwellings, shops and inns dotted the countryside. In the distance, livestock and farm houses with green fields in the background completed the rural scene.

The country air, flowers, green paddocks and livestock reminded him of his early years in England. John wondered what a posting to a Victorian country district would be like. Did he have the necessary experience to be able to be effective outside the cover of the Police Headquarters' umbrella? If he didn't – how could he get it?

John decided at the first opportunity, he would make an appointment to speak with Sub Inspector Alford, his senior officer, to get his opinion.

John felt comfortable with Sub Officer Alford. He was one of the original Victorian Police Officers and had previously served with the Liverpool Police. He gave clear orders and his expectations were realistic and achievable.

When John met with him he was greeted with a smile. "Well, Williams, what's this all about? I hope you're not leaving?"

"Well yes and no, sir," John replied. "I would like your opinion on my qualifications for a posting to a country district."

The officer nodded. "Williams, you are probably the best sergeant in the Metropolitan Police.

"To answer – you are already qualified. The Commissioner is looking for your type right now. I don't wish to lose you but I won't stand in your way. Put your application in and I will support your request. You should go far in the force." He stood up and shook John's hand.

John was surprised and delighted with his immediate response. "Thank you, sir." He submitted his application the next day.

The daily briefings were carried out by the Duty Sub Inspector. He read out the events that had occurred overnight, details of possible culprits and the day's allocated tasks. John made notes of these instructions. Who knew, they could help him and his constables arrest a culprit or two!

John was surprised at the lack of interest shown by several constables. *If I ever make Duty Sub Inspector, I will change that attitude in my staff,* he thought.

His country posting application was acknowledged and it was all John could do to wait for an interview. Their daily patrols were always unpredictable, which kept them on their toes. Although John's thoughts were elsewhere, he remained alert on duty.

A routine escort to Pentridge Stockade that went wrong created a new challenge for him. When the daily load of twenty prisoners was being unloaded at the side gates of the Stockade in the early evening, six prisoners escaped.

The Stockade enclosed a collection of wooden buildings with two heavy side gates which required two warders to open and close each gate. After the prisoners were unloaded and the wardens were attempting to close one gate, a hinge snapped and the gate tilted. The prisoners saw their chance and made a dash for freedom.

During the resulting melee, most prisoners were stopped but six got away through the tilted gate. One escapee was captured within the hour but the other five were seen to split into two groups.

One group consisted of two escapees and the second group of three escapees, each heading in a north westerly direction into the thick forest. A rider was immediately sent to Melbourne to inform Police Headquarters.

The next morning the Commissioner called a meeting with his senior officers and instructed them to form search teams, concentrating on the roads to the gold fields and to inform the Geelong Barracks, Cobb and Co. Coaches and the Police Gold escorts.

These officers then assembled all available police on duty at the barracks. A Senior Inspector read out the records and descriptions of the five escapees. John recorded their tattoos, scars and other visible means of identification, in his notebook. One was a murderer, two were thieves and the remaining two were thugs.

It was presumed they would head either to Ballarat or Bendigo and mingle with the many hundreds of would-be miners travelling to the goldfields.

Some were riding in coaches, or on horseback. Many more were walking, pushing wheel barrows or carrying picks and odds and ends over their shoulder. The escapees could easily blend in with the mass of travellers.

The Senior Inspector decided to have three teams, each headed by a Sub Inspector with a sergeant and four constables. Two Inspectors were to proceed to Campbellfield and Keilor and organise the local police and community.

It was decided to send one team to Coburg and head on a zig zagging course in a westerly direction towards the Keilor Plains.

A second team would head to Campbellfield, in case the escapees headed north to the Heathcote goldfields and then head to Bulla. The road north from Bulla joined the Bendigo road five miles further on.

A third team was to proceed direct to Keilor Plains via Essendon. Keilor was the junction of the two main roads to Ballarat and Bendigo. This was John's team.

The Senior Inspector said he wanted the teams to be comprised of men with country police service experience, or men recruited from the country. "We don't want to have to send out search parties looking for lost constables. Your task requires you use your initiative and spread out to cover as much country as you see fit. Speak with farmers and any locals you encounter." Finally he said, "You are to be ready to leave within the hour. Good luck."

Sub Inspector Alford selected John, ignoring the Inspector's order. He also selected his two constables plus two new constables to complete his team. He felt comfortable with the team. The two new constables were enthusiastic and from the country.

Fortunately John had spent a few hours each week horse riding and was now reasonably proficient, although not up to the standard of the new constables.

After receiving some supplies, firearms and ammunition, the teams assembled at the stables. The horses had been feed and watered and the ostler had made sure the horses were sound and their shoes were secure. After they saddled them they doubled checked their harness straps and buckles were in good condition.

John and the Sub Inspector were each armed with a revolver. Two constables were equipped with shotguns and the other two with carbines. They left the Melbourne Barracks on the hour heading north to Essendon.

The team left the barracks early afternoon looking forward to the challenge they faced. Melbourne was founded just over twenty years ago and many local districts had only recently been settled. The majority of these districts were covered with dense forests, as were the areas in the district they were to search. Water courses and deep ravines would also test their riding skills.

When they stopped for a break at Essendon, several bystanders approached them. "Is it true that there has been a mass outbreak of prisoners from Pentridge Stockade?"

Sub Inspector Alford conducted a meeting in the local inn to advise the actual situation. He explained that it was considered the five escapees would avoid populated districts and head further north towards the goldfields.

The listeners were pleased to hear this commentary and nodded in agreement with this logic. The Sub Inspector hoped he was correct. After a complimentary meal from the inn owner, the team headed to Keilor where they arrived after night fall.

At Keilor they were unable to find accommodation and ended up bedding down in the police stables. It was comfortable, dry and they all slept deeply, even John who was saddle sore. He was reminded he was in the country when he was awakened by a loudly crowing rooster an hour before dawn.

The following morning, they met the local constabulary, a sergeant and two constables. It was agreed the locals would remain in Keilor and the Sub Inspector's team would search the surrounding district.

It was a heavily treed area with plenty of wildlife. The tree branches were filled with various coloured birds with pleasant calls. They saw kangaroos lying under the trees or hopping along with long bounds. The sun was shining and there was only a slight breeze. It was an excellent day to be out riding – albeit searching.

Sub Inspector Alford split them into two groups – John with his two constables and he with the other two constables. John was to head north for three hours, turn east for three hours then return to Keilor. Sub Inspector Alford would head in the opposite direction.

If they located an escapee they were to fire two carbine shots. Most of the day they would be near enough to hear their carbine shots. They were to visit any farms they came close to and have a brief chat with the tenants seeking information and advising them to be alert. Most would have dogs to alert them to any strangers.

The first two days they visited every farm house on their path and spoke with the tenants. Several said they had heard their dogs barking at night but had seen no one. They continued searching without luck, slightly varying their search area each day.

On the third day they had been riding for two hours when they came across a man sitting by a creek, fishing, He was obviously hard up. John greeted the man. "Good morning." The man nodded but didn't reply.

John continued. "We're searching for some escaped convicts. There may be two or three. Have you seen any people in the bush lately?"

The man nodded and pointed up the creek but did not talk.

"How many?" John asked.

The man held up three fingers.

John was now both excited and frustrated. He

pulled a shilling from his pocket and showed it to the man.

The man immediately stood up and put his hand out for the coin. "They are about two miles up the creek and in a bad way. They are starving. I saw them this morning."

John gave him the coin.

They headed alongside the creek, wending their way through the thick bushes. The horses were noisy and were taking too long getting through the underbrush so John decided to dismount and leave the horses.

He left Constable Lane with the horses and headed upstream with Constable Smith. Within ten minutes they heard voices.

John drew his pistol and crept forward. Immediately in front of him were two convicts sitting in a clearing under a tree. They were in poor shape. Their clothes were torn and dirty and their cheap prison shoes had split. John looked for the third man but could not see him. He nodded to Constable Smith and they both stepped into the clearing.

John said, "Surrender in the Queen's name."

The escapees just sat there, stunned, offering no resistance.

"Where is the third man?" John asked.

They both shook the heads and one said, "He left us this morning."

Constable Smith handcuffed the two escapees together and the four of them headed back to the horses and Constable Lane.

When they arrived back at the horses, Constable Lane was smiling. "Where's the third one?"

John answered, wondering what had made Lane smile. "I don't know. He seems to have got away."

"No, he didn't. I've got him. He's over there under

the tree. He was crashing through the bushes and walked right into me. When he saw me he just collapsed, exhausted. It was a very easy arrest." Constable Lane's smile was now explained.

"We couldn't get any food because of the bloody farm dogs." the escapee said. Ironically he was the murderer.

After they fed the escapees from their daily rations they commenced the slow trip back to base.

John was elated. They had captured three of the escapees on the third day of searching. He fired the two alerting carbine shots and the answering two shots were judged to be close.

John cut short the planned search area and headed on an intercept course to join with the Sub Inspector's track and then head back to Keilor. They spotted the Sub Inspector's team on a hilltop and soon joined them.

Sub Inspector Alford was delighted with their success and sent one of his constables to advise the Melbourne Barracks of the capture.

The next morning Sub Inspector Alford was debating whether to proceed to Bulla and assist the other two teams, when he heard of a constable from Bulla who was riding to the Melbourne Barracks to inform them that the other two escapees were also in custody. They had surrendered voluntarily to the Bulla Police Station, exhausted and starving.

Later it was revealed that they were unable to obtain food or replace their prison uniforms. Like the three John had captured, the dogs at the farms had kept them away from the gardens, orchards and clotheslines.

John's three escapees were held in the Keilor lockup. They soon recovered, after meals, a wash and fresh clothes. One escapee in particular recovered very well and was soon up to his old tricks.

The Constable and the Miner

Within the week he had escaped from his lockup due to the inattention of the duty warder – himself a former Tasmanian convict. As the escapee was only a minor thief it was decided that he did not warrant wasting any further manpower or expenditure on and that was the end of the matter. He just vanished, probably mingling with miners in the goldfields.

On their return to the Melbourne Barracks, the Commissioner spoke at an assembly and praised the speed and efficiency of the three teams and made special mention of Sub Inspector Alford's team. Each member of the team had an entry made on their file noting their exemplary performance.

John's family knew he had been sent to search for the escapees but were surprised to learn of his role in the capture of some of the criminals. Surprisingly Jane was calm and accepted the drama stoically.

Around this time, the newspapers were mounting a campaign against the Melbourne innkeepers. They maintained these establishments were out of control and were a menace to the general public. Brawls and noise were continuing every night, regardless of the number of times the innkeepers were fined. The fines were only a few pounds and the innkeepers could make ten times that amount in a single night. When their annual license came up for renewal it was renewed regardless of the number of times they had broken the law.

The law needed to be amended. Something had to be done. Raise the fines or deny renewal of a repeat offender's license? But who was going to initiate this legal amendment? A Member of Parliament? Not likely!

After an incident involving a drunken lout trying to enter a coach with a senior government official and his wife on board and abusing them, the Commissioner was instructed to do something immediately about this community problem.

Previously the police arrested offenders and gaoled them overnight and released them after a magistrate or a justice of the peace imposed a fine. This was a reoccurring event, day after day.

The major contributor to this problem was the liquor license renewal system. It was seen as a routine action without controls or standards. The majority of licenses were renewed by justices of the peace without reference to licensees' observance, or otherwise, of the strict requirements of the Liquor Act. Unfortunately the judiciary was being corrupted with rampant bribery.

A meeting was held of all inspectors and sergeants. The Senior Inspector spoke at length about the law, the innkeepers and their customers. But he only repeated what everyone in the room already knew.

"Don't expect the Law to change in the immediate future. We must come up with a tactic to at least reduce the problem."

Several ideas were floated and rejected.

John stood up. "If we concentrate our patrols nightly only on the most disreputable inns near residential areas, we could drive the worst drunks out of that area. They will get sick and tired of being gaoled and fined and will leave. Importantly, it will be a visible improvement to the community.

"Ignore the wharf district for the time being, as it is not a residential area and is a lower priority. The drunks are happy to fight each other; leave them to it. They're only a problem to themselves." Nods of agreement by his peers pleased John, and he sat down.

The Senior Inspector stood up. "This seems to be a plan to consider. I will put it to the Commissioner."

He paused. "Anyone else wish to speak? No one? Thank you." He turned and left the room. Several smiled and acknowledged John as they left.

Later that day, Sub Inspector Alford went to see John. "I knew that you would have an idea. Well done. The Commissioner has accepted your plan. It starts tonight."

Professional men frequented their clubs and were not a problem. The members handled any members who offended. The inns were classified into three groups. The first group contained the few which were well run and frequented by tradesmen. The second group was the targeted disreputable inns and the third were the inns at the wharf. Most inns were in dingy surroundings, badly lit streets and poorly built. Some inns had bare floors.

The better inns had carpets or mats, slab walls with a similar roof, together with a wooden bar table with stools and chairs that were crudely made but plentiful. The inns were required by law to have lighting – however poor.

On the first morning of the plan's implementation, the cells were filled with drunks from the previous night's patrol, all from the second group of inns.

The cells continued to be filled daily for the next two weeks. During the third week there was a noticeable decline in the number of offenders in the cells in the mornings. John's plan was working.

However the plan had some detractors. Eighteen inns had been targeted. Sixteen innkeepers had enough of the extra police attention and changed their attitude to drunks, but two were decidedly unhappy. Coincidently they were two of the worst offenders with their drunken and noisy customers and were not happy to see some of their best drinkers leave. They wrote to the newspapers alleging victimisation. Their letters were published but they received no support whatsoever from the community. They then wrote to the local Member of Parliament who acknowledged receipt of the letter and then did nothing. Finally they accepted the inevitable and 'Cleaned up their act'.

Another complaint came from within the police department. Murders had increased in the wharf area and were stretching their resources. After a period of three months the numbers of murders and serious crime had been reduced by half. The reason was never proved but perhaps the purge of the other innkeepers was indirectly responsible.

After their success in the residential areas, it was decided to carry out ad hoc mounted patrols in the wharfs district in the early morning when it was still dark. This was always a risky patrol. The drunks did not like horses. Some even jumped into the river when the horses appeared out of the dark. The mounted constables often remained on horseback with their batons drawn.

It was usual to make no arrests but many inn patrons had sore heads and bruised arms after a dawn police patrol visit. When the not-so-drunk patrons heard the horses approaching they quickly vanished into the darkness to avoid the baton. As the constables said, "It saves paperwork." John wasn't sure he agreed, but the baton definitely helped to reduce the problem.

The patrols had not completely stopped the drunken behaviour but it contained the worse of it to an area that the general community avoided. The Commissioner considered this a satisfactory outcome while the license renewal debacle continued.

John wondered what the country innkeepers were like, and how they were controlled by the Land

Commissioners who were responsible for Liquor Licenses outside of the Melbourne District.

The reduction of complaints regarding drunken behaviour was duly reported in the newspapers and had the Commissioner smiling. He posted a letter on the notice board acknowledging the success of the plan. He also wrote John a letter of commendation. He had become well known in the police force.

Melbourne was still growing out of control, while the countryside was quickly being developed with farming and grazing properties reaching to the Murray River and beyond across to west Victoria. Livestock was being droved from Sydney to Victoria and South Australia, and explorers were heading north, seeking to be the first to cross the continent.

There were more reports of gold being discovered on the outskirts of Melbourne and this was also generating manpower problems with many employers struggling to provide services when their staff suddenly decided to become miners and seek their fortunes. It was an exciting time for John and his family to see the Colony unfold.

Jane was content with her lot. She had established a small vegetable garden with flowers around the small cottage. She, George and Sarah had made friends and had a pet dog called Rusty. Its breed was unknown. It had short hair, was thick set and followed Jane everywhere and was inclined to be a bit protective. Rusty bailed up a messenger one day, who had to stay very still in the front garden until George came home an hour later.

Two weeks after his forty-third birthday John received a letter informing him that he was being posted to Kyneton and was to take up the posting at the end of the month – ten days' time. John had heard of Kyneton.

He knew that it was a developing farming centre about fifty miles north of Melbourne on the Campaspe River.

Jane received the news quietly. She knew that John had applied for a posting to a country town and now it had happened. George and Sarah listened while their parents discussed the move. It was decided that Jane and the children would stay in Melbourne for the time being. George was working at the Australia Hotel as a desk clerk and Sarah was employed by Mrs Jones, a dress designer who had a small shop in Collins Street. Both were content with their lives and had formed friendships. They wanted to stay in Melbourne. As John was unaware what accommodation was available in Kyneton, there was no question of Jane going with him yet.

The next day John met with Sub Inspector Alford, who congratulated him. He motioned him to be seated. The Sub Inspector handed John an envelope which contained a briefing of the Kyneton District, together with a list of the local organisations and the names of notable identities.

"You will have two horses supplied for your use, together with riding gear and pack horse equipment. Accommodation is a problem. You can stay in an hotel until you find something suitable. I've been to Kyneton and I can assure you that you will enjoy the district. It is halfway between Melbourne and the Bendigo goldfields, is a growing farming centre and serviced by the stage coach company, Cobb and Co. They run ten coaches each day, five each way – three by day and two by night. The people are friendly and the scenery excellent. You definitely will enjoy the posting. I will be sorry to lose you but you will gain more experience in a country police station and I feel sure that you will progress up the promotional ladder. Hand these papers to District

Inspector Brittan; they are your records. In case I do not see you before you go, I wish you all the best and no doubt we will meet again. Good bye for now."

John was given seven days leave of absence from police duty before he needed to leave.

Before he left, he and Jane walked into Melbourne from Richmond. It was a pleasant summer day with the sun shining and birds aplenty. They headed to the river bank and strolled arm in arm along the grassy slope. The river was crammed with small boats going in all directions. The large sailing ships could not navigate the river and anchored in Hobsons Bay some four miles downriver, to the west of Melbourne, and their passengers were ferried, in small river boats and barges, up river to the township of Melbourne.

Melbourne was less than twenty years old and its growth had been rapid. Governor Bourke had named it after Lord Melbourne in 1837. It was about a mile square with a small gully extending through the middle. Most streets were only tracks with potholes everywhere. Only the main streets had been formed and gravelled.

John mused about what the lower streets in the gully would be like after heavy rain.

Immigrant ships were arriving every day, and new shops opening weekly. On the south side of the river there was a canvas village. Accommodation demands could not keep up with the influx of immigrants. The town planning was haphazard. Buildings varied from bluestone edifices alongside hovels to vacant blocks. The river was fouled and the town smelt.

John was happy to be leaving Melbourne and would miss his family but he looked forward to enjoying the country air and his new position.

CHAPTER FOUR

Lucks A Fortune

Was it smoke or dust that he could see rising from behind the hill? He had heard a violent noise and turned in its direction. Could it be the mine? He started to run towards the hill. Horsemen were already galloping past him. He looked down at the mine and, through the clouds of dust billowing from the entrance, he could see people milling around it. What had happened?

Sean Hogan had worked here as a miner for the last three years and had friends working there today. The closer he got, the more fearful he became. No one had entered the shaft yet. They were waiting for the dust to stop and settle. He stopped next to a fellow miner. "Do you know what happened?"

The miner looked at him with a shocked expression and shook his head, not answering.

The dust settled within an hour. The supervisor then organised a team of miners to follow him into the mine shaft. They were only gone for ten minutes when they all returned, looking grim.

The supervisor stood on a bench and addressed

the anxious crowd. "The shaft shoring has collapsed about fifty feet in and the tunnel is full of rocks and soil and it's still very unstable. We will try to dig in and erect new timbers to shore up the tunnel but we will need to be careful. We will start now. We need to form a line starting with men shoring, men digging and men to fill the hand trucks and men to move the hand trucks and dump the debris."

He pointed to selected men. "You, you and you get some timber for shoring. You three gather some shovels and picks." He issued orders until he had organised his workforce. They all moved quickly to carry out the grim task.

Sean moved to a hand truck and started to push it into the shaft. Unfortunately within ten minutes another fall occurred and nearly trapped five of the assigned diggers. The work had to be stopped.

The shaft had been dug at ground level into the corner of a high hill. The supervisor and the more senior miners huddled together and spoke quietly amongst themselves. Sean wondered what else they could do. Dig into the shaft?

Nearly all the wives and families of the miners had arrived by now. The scene was chaotic with their crying and screaming.

Sean wished he was elsewhere. He had the feeling that there was nothing that could be done for the trapped miners. The supervisor stepped up to the bench again. He stood there for a while, not saying a word. He appeared hesitant to speak. Looking at the families, one could understand why.

He cleared his throat. "I'll be honest with you, we will try to dig into the tunnel from another direction but it will take time. We know that the tunnel is unstable as you can see from the depression in the area further up the hill, immediately above the collapsed tunnel section. We will start digging now with the afternoon shift. Also we need to do a check of the miners who were on the day shift."

After the day shift name check was completed, twelve miners were identified as missing. This caused some rejoicing but also anguish for the families of the missing miners. Sean did not know them personally.

Sean was sent home and told to report to the mine early next morning to take his turn digging the new tunnel. Still in shock, he sat quietly thinking. What if he had been working at the time of the tunnel collapse?

He had born in Cumberland in the North of England. After a few years of schooling he had joined his father in his blacksmith's shop. His job had been to collect horses and ride them to the smithy and return them to their owners after they were shod. He also helped to work the forge and repair saddles and harnesses.

His mother had died when he was young and when his father passed on he sold the blacksmith shop. His few possessions he packed into a quality leather bag he had made and the twenty sovereigns he received from the sale of the shop, he sewed into compartments in a matching leather money belt.

Sean wandered the county until he decided to settle in this small mining town and become a miner. The mine was a large iron ore deposit. Although the mining work was demanding, his time working for his father as an apprentice blacksmith had made him a strong and fit young man. He soon blended into the workforce.

The next morning he reported for work and helped to continue to dig the rescue tunnel. This continued for three days until this shaft collapsed beneath the diggers. Fortunately the three diggers who fell with the collapse were rescued.

This incident caused the rescue mission to be

stopped. Rightly or wrongly this was the decision made by the mine owners, much to the shock of families of the buried miners.

The owners then abandoned the site completely, thus causing further grief for the employment of the remaining miners and their families. Apart from the trauma they had all endured – they were now jobless.

The mood around the village quickly changed from contentment to gloom, with many departing.

Sean also decided to leave. It was easy for him to go as he had no ties. After a few ales with his friends he left the district. He was now twenty-four years of age. Where to go? What to do?

He decided to travel again and headed north to the Port of Liverpool to seek a job or a berth on a ship to go somewhere, anywhere.

Sean still had the sovereigns in his belt and some pay from the mine but preferred to walk and carry his leather bag. At times he was given a ride on the back of a cart or dray. He enjoyed the countryside. It was typical English farm land, lush and green, with livestock quietly grazing. Birds were plentiful and happily chirping away, with colourful flowers and scrubs completing the scene. He arrived at the Liverpool docks at sunset and went looking for an inn to stay the night.

He was strolling towards the lights of an inn when he heard a loud fearful cry for help. Three figures appeared in front of him. A small man was being attacked by two others. Sean dropped his leather bag, grabbed the nearest one of the attackers by the neck and waist and threw him bodily across the road.

The other attacker turned his attention to him and threw a punch that glanced off Sean's shoulder. Sean swung his arm and smacked him hard on the side of his face with the open palm of his hand and knocked the assailant off his feet. He sat groggily on the ground for a moment then got up and ran off, his mate following him.

The person who had been attacked was leaning against a wall. He looked at Sean. "Thank you. I was in trouble. They tried to rob me. They were too strong. You came along at the right time." He took a deep breath. "My name's Tom." They shook hands.

"I'm Sean. They were cowards. I'm glad you were not harmed. You look as if you could do with an ale?"

Tom nodded agreement and they walked into the nearby inn.

The inn was typical for an English Port. Maritime memorabilia hung on the walls and over the bar. It looked rough but was comfortable. They sat near a window with a view of the moored ships. Tom had a large bruise below his left eye and the eye had partly closed. They sat quietly and made small talk.

Then Tom pointed, looking out of the window. "See that tall ship with the three masts. That's mine. I'm the Sail Master. We have been in port for a week and we sail on the morning tide."

Sean was surprised that the sailing ship was so big. With its complex of rope ladders and with the many other single ropes it was a most impressive sight. He guessed that the sails were the canvas folds tied to the wooden cross beams.

Sean asked straight out, "How does one become a sailor? I came to Liverpool to join a ship to see the world. I have only seen the northern English counties. I have worked as a miner, and a blacksmith. I can ride a horse and mend saddles and bridles but I know nothing about ships or sailing."

Tom looked at Sean. "I can see that you have been a blacksmith. You showed your strength when you struck that thug with your open hand. You may have broken his jaw." Sean just shrugged his shoulders. "You mentioned that you repaired saddles and harnesses." Sean nodded. "Exactly what repairs did you do?"

"I replaced the stuffing in the saddle seat and any stitches that had broken or were badly worn and were ready to break, also on harnesses and bridles," Sean replied and waited for him to comment.

"Last week I lost my assistant overboard. I don't know how, so don't ask." He paused, looking at Sean's leather bag. "Did you make this bag? What size needles did you use to repair the harnesses stitching?"

Sean shook his head. He didn't know the needle size. "Yes, I made the bag from calf skin. It lasts much longer than other materials. It takes longer to sew but it's worth the extra effort." Tom picked up the leather bag, examined it closely and was impressed with the workmanship.

Tom looked hard at Sean, summing him up, thinking he would make a good assistant in the sail locker. "It's too late to get you signed on as a crew member now but I can smuggle you on board and you can sleep in the sail locker. When we are at sea I'll take you to the bosun to see if he will let me have you as my assistant." He paused. "I think he will. I know how he thinks. He'd rather have a working sailor on board than a stowaway in the brig. This is my chance to repay you for your help. Are you interested?"

Sean sat there, surprised, trying to absorb what Tom had just said. He had been offered a job on a sailing ship and he had been in Liverpool for only a few hours. He had not anticipated this situation occurring. He sat there for a few seconds and then impetuously reached across the table and shook Tom's hand. "Yes, thank you, Tom. I'll come along."

Sean followed Tom down the pier to the ship. It seemed to get bigger as he got closer.

A watch keeper was on duty at the top of the gangway. Tom nodded to him and told him Sean was with him. The watch keeper just nodded. Tom continued to walk to the bow and entered a small hatchway. Three levels of ladders took them down to the sail locker. It had a low ceiling and had long narrow side sections where the spare sails were stowed. They stopped in front of a long narrow table. Sean could see this was where damaged sails were repaired.

Two wooden beams were suspended from the ceiling from which sailors' hammocks were slung. Tom pointed to a rolled up hammock. "You can have that one. It belonged to my previous assistant. He has no use for it now. I sleep over the table. You can sling your hammock by the starboard bulkhead."

Sean looked at him, confused.

Tom smiled and continued. "Face the bow; that's the sharp end of the ship. Starboard and green are on your right and port and red are on your left. Don't forget these words of wisdom."

Sean was shown how to sling his hammock to the beams and after several attempts, he managed to swing up and lower himself into it. He found that it was uncomfortable and fumbled around behind him. In the blanket he found a loaded revolver. He placed it in his belt and did not tell Tom.

Surprisingly, he slept deeply until Tom woke him by shaking his shoulder. He told him to stay in the sail locker and when he returned he would bring him some food. Sean could hear activity above him, running, shouting, bells, whistles and other unfamiliar noises.

Sean had no idea of the time. He heard the ship's bell ring several times but it meant nothing to Sean. Over the next weeks he would learn the number of rings of the bell indicted the time of the day and night in hours.

It was rung every four hours to advise the start or the end of a duty watch and in the evening it was rung once at a two hour interval, between the dog watches.

While waiting for Tom to return, he examined the revolver. It was new, of the latest design and loaded with six balls and caps. He decided that the best place to hide it would be where he found it, in the blanket. He rolled it up in his hammock and stowed it under a sail locker.

While waiting impatiently for Tom and his promised meal, he began to feel the ship swaying. He was finally sailing – but to where? Sean suddenly realised that Tom had not told him the ship's destination. He sat there quietly laughing to himself. *What a great way to start my new life. I hope I've made a good decision.*

Tom eventually arrived with the promised food – some bread and cheese. He said that the ship was now in the Irish Sea heading south.

Sean interrupted. "You haven't told me the ship's destination yet. Where are we going?"

Tom answered, "Sorry about that. I thought I had. We are going to Sydney in New South Wales via Rio de Janeiro in Brazil and Cape Town in South Africa. After Sydney we will return via the Cape of Good Hope. Our ship will average about two hundred and forty miles a day. We will be away for most of the year."

"That's a long time," Sean replied, surprised.

"If you keep busy, it soon passes and after a week or two at sea we will be kept busy, repairing sail eyelets and sometimes the sails themselves need patching," Tom explained. "Let's meet the bosun."

Tom took him up a narrow ladder and forward along the main deck. Sean looked around in amazement when he saw the amount of rope in use. It was everywhere. He would soon learn that a sailing ship comprised wood, canvas and rope.

A tall lean suntanned sailor was looking at them as they approached.

He looked at Tom and asked, "Don't tell me that you have already found a replacement for that useless bastard you lost overboard?" The bosun did not smile. He just glared at them both.

Tom was undaunted by his attitude. "He is strong and can sew and it wasn't my fault I lost my assistant, Bosun."

The bosun asked abruptly, "Have you been to sea before?"

Sean thought before he replied. *Maybe I'm in trouble.* He shook his head. "No, but I can learn like anyone else has to when they first go to sea." That was a good answer.

The bosun stared at him, then back at Tom. "Take him to the purser and sign him on." He then turned and walked away.

Tom was smiling and shook Sean's hand. "Good. I'll put you to work."

The ship continued south for a few weeks then headed to Rio de Janiero. The seas were calm and Sean soon gained his sea legs. The rolling and pitching of a ship makes a person step lightly and feel for the deck, much different than walking normally on a stable surface.

As Tom had said, they were soon repairing the sails' eyelets through which the ropes, holding the corners of the sails, were threaded and tied to the yardarm. The continuous buffeting of the winds on the sails created stress at the corners of the sails where the eyelets were attached and seams of the canvas sections. The sails had shrouds across them to reduce the sails from flapping and helped spread the stress but still sails split and required repairing.

Sean soon found that repairing canvas was no different than repairing a saddle or harness except that a sail repair required more space in which to work. He made himself a leather palm glove to help push the needle through canvas. It was the same technique he had used for saddle and harness leather repairs.

Tom was happy with Sean's skills and he found that he was not as overworked as he had been with his previous assistant, who was really only a labourer with no specific skills.

The bosun visited the sail locker unexpectedly, stood and watched as Sean was repairing a split sail. After about five minutes he left without commenting. As Sean found out later, that was a good sign. You only had to worry if he decided to say something to you.

They sailed into Rio de Janiero harbour on a bright sunny morning. The large sandy beach and the surrounding hills, together with the mountain peak in the background, made it look inviting to visit. But neither Tom nor Sean went ashore, there was too much work to do. All the sails had to be inspected and repaired as required, with the lines stowed or cheesed ready for use.

The ship was supplied with fresh water, fruit and meat and other essentials. They sailed on the next tide. They had a long voyage in front of them across the South Atlantic Ocean to Cape Town then on to the Cape of Good Hope via Sydney in the Colony of New South Wales. The seas would soon be rougher with stronger winds. Sean would soon become a real sailor.

The ship ploughed into the seas with the bow dipping and creating large sprays of water surging into the air almost covering the ship. The Captain had half of the sails furled to reduce the speed of the ship. A strong wind was blowing from the west and directly astern. They were making good time.

Sean had been assigned to a deck crew to help handle the furling or reefing of the sails, depending on the wind strength. His hands and wrists were chaffed by the salt and water on the halyard ropes and the sails. He had to climb the rope ratlines several times to adjust a top halyard. The pitching and rolling of the ship had him holding on for dear life several times. He later said that he found it exhilarating, but would only do it again if ordered. He would not be volunteering.

They had been sailing for three weeks. The seas had abated and the wind was steady. Most crew enjoyed a day or two of leisure.

Not the sail makers; they worked on the sails. During the rough seas, sails had been damaged. As normal the eyelets; they were easily repaired. The most difficult repairs were the tears along the sail's canvas joining seams. The sail locker was small and the sail needed to be unfolded in very cramped space. The bosun would visit and say nothing other than grunt and would walk on. Sean took this as an acceptance of their skills.

They glided into Cape Town Harbour on an incoming tide with a gentle following breeze. It was a beautiful day, with the sun shining on the face of Table Mountain which dominated the background of the town.

The Captain said that he was sailing on the next outgoing tide. He was only stopping to take on fresh food and water and not exchanging any cargo.

Tom and John decided to have a couple of hours ashore to stretch their legs.

For a person who had never been to a foreign country before, it was an education for Sean. The majority of the wharf hands were African natives – strong, healthy with shiny ebony skin. They laughed and joked as they worked.

Sean was impressed. The dock side had rows and rows of warehouses and several open markets. The tourists were well served with general shops selling artefacts, gaudy clothes and local weapons.

Some of the customs officers spoke with a strong Dutch accent. This was the first time he had heard it.

He asked Tom, "Is Australia going to be different, like here?"

Tom smiled. "Yes and no. I'll tell you later what to expect. Let's head back to the ship. We don't have much time left."

The bosun was on the gangway. "I was wondering where you two were. Get below. We're sailing on the hour."

The ship left the harbor as planned and headed due east to cross the vast Indian Ocean to the Australian Colonies and Sean's future. He had not told Tom he was intending to leave the ship in Sydney. His future was on the land, not on the high seas.

When they were at sea again, Sean asked Tom, "What did you mean 'yes and no' when we were ashore?"

"Australia has its own natives called Aborigines but the day to day language is almost all English. It's controlled by the British Colonial Office through an appointed Governor. The country is booming with immigration and gold rushes. There are plenty of opportunities for people like you. It's not for me. I've been at sea for too long. When I settle down it will be in an English port town. I would still want to smell the sea," Tom answered.

The winds were prevailing westerly and gusting. The seas were choppy, white caps were visible as far as the eye could see. The ship was making good way, even with these conditions. The clouds looked to be threatening rain.

The same weather continued for over three weeks. It was to be expected that the sail makers would eventually be busy. The mizzen sail was the first to let go. With a resounding rip, the sail split in two. The bosun soon had all hands furling the remaining sections and had it taken to the sail locker. A replacement sail was rigged within the watch.

The two sail sections were rolled with the torn edges on the outside. Starting from one side Tom and Sean started to sew the edges together. It was demanding work. The sail sections were wet and the sea water salt soon made their hands and fingers red and painful. The repair to join the mizzen sail took all day. That night at mess time they had trouble eating their meals, their hands were so sore.

The next sail failure was the top most mainsail. The top corner eyelet appeared to have torn away and the sail was flapping violently, so the crew furled the entire sail. As the ship was making such good time the Captain decided to leave it on the yardarm and to continue with the remaining sails.

The bosun came down to the sail locker and accused Tom and Sean of shoddy work and said he was going to dock their pay by half. Tom was furious and Sean was shocked. The bosun turned and walked out of the locker.

Tom immediately said, "I'm leaving this ship in Sydney. This is the second time in four voyages he has accused the sail makers of shoddy work and docked our pay. I've had enough. I'm leaving. I can easily get another ship."

Sean had his sovereigns in his belt and he had already decided to leave the ship. He now told Tom he was leaving as well. The remainder of the voyage was without drama. The bosun did not approach them again.

The coastal mountain range of Tasmania was the first Australian land Sean saw, as it appeared out of an early morning mist. It looked forbidding with its dense green foliage and dark grey escarpments. There were a few wisps of smoke but no evidence of a settlement. The ship tracked south to sail around the Tasmanian coast and then headed north to Sydney.

Sean saw the coast of New South Wales two days before they arrived at Port Jackson – albeit Sydney Cove. The coastline consisted of rugged cliffs interrupted by sandy beaches with cottages and farms, grazing livestock and forests vanishing into the distance. Their ship sailed past small fishing boats who gave them a friendly wave. Sean was starting to feel comfortable with his decision to travel. Some long beaches had high rolling waves crashing onto their shores.

They sailed into Port Jackson on top of the tide. The small opening was between the two massive rocky cliffs and belied the size of the enormous harbor. The cliffs were home to all sorts of birds who flew in colourful wheeling formations making an awful din. One side of the opening was named South Head where there was a lighthouse and signal station. The other side was North Head where a quarantine station had been established. Both sides of the harbour had many bays and inlets with dwellings throughout their foreshores and up into the nearby hills. Sydney Cove was growing. The waters were occupied with all types of ships crossing between the harbour's foreshores.

The ship's sails were furled and it slowly lost way. It was then towed sideways by two large row boats until ropes were thrown to wharf labourers who pulled the ship alongside a long wharf to join rows of other ships. Government officials came on board to perform their required duty and to eagerly seek news from England and any old newspapers or journals.

The crew lined up for their pay, overseen by the bosun.

Tom and Sean were paid half as advised by the bosun, who stupidly said, "That will teach you two to do better on the way back to Liverpool."

Just then the crew chief walked up, holding a rope. "The eyelet on the top mainsail didn't fail; this rope came lose. There was nothing wrong with the sail."

Tom and Sean went back to the sail locker, collected their bags and unobtrusively threw them down onto the wharf behind some cargo. They walked past an unsmiling bosun, who was watching to see if they were taking their bags ashore and intending to desert. He would find out when he was ready to sail, that his two sailmakers had indeed deserted. The two picked up their bags from behind the cargo on the wharf and walked into Sydney town. When the Captain found out the reason the ship was sailing without any sail makers, he replaced the bosun with his deputy. No one had won.

CHAPTER FIVE

A New Life

Sydney town had not been planned; it had 'happened'. The streets were narrow, cluttered with rubbish and smelt of rotting vegetation and worse. The buildings ranged from magnificent sandstone government offices to slums all within a mile square. However there were some beautiful green areas with grand views of the harbor, which had vessels of all sizes churning up the waters.

They walked up from the dock area to a small inn and paid for two bunks in a large dormitory. They enjoyed a meal of fresh ham and eggs with tea. The bedding was reasonably clean but the other patrons appeared somewhat disreputable so Sean used his bag as a pillow.

Early in the morning he was woken by a callow youth pointing a knife at him and demanding money. Sean asked to be allowed to sit up. When he did, he put his hand into the front of trousers as if he was going to give the robber some money. Instead he drew out his revolver and levelled it between the robber's eyes without saying a word.

The youth's reaction was a scream, "Don't shoot," followed by his rapid exit from the dormitory. Tom looked at Sean, said nothing, rolled over and went back to sleep as if nothing had happened.

The next day the two said goodbye. Sean thanked Tom for getting him to Sydney and wished him well on his return to the sea. Tom went to find a ship and Sean went to find a job – any job! He walked down the main street, enjoying looking in the shop windows. He had been a sailor for nearly four months but had missed the life he had previously known.

The next day during a stroll, he saw a sign on an inn notice board asking for volunteers to join a cattle herd moving overland, from Sydney to Melbourne. Needed were skilled stockmen, a cook, a farrier-blacksmith and general rouseabouts. The hirer was staying at this inn. His name was Maluka.

Sean nervously entered the rowdy bar and asked for Maluka. The barman pointed to a corner table where two men sat talking. The taller of the two saw him approaching and nodded.

"I'm looking for Maluka," Sean said.

"That's me. What can I do for you? Are you after a job?"

"Yes I'm a farrier and blacksmith and I'm interested in doing something different, such as travelling overland to Melbourne," Sean replied.

Maluka nodded to him to sit down. "Tell me your background and we'll see. This is my head stockman."

About an hour later, after much questioning from both men and from Sean, he had the job as the farrier, answerable only to Maluka. The agreed terms were; he had to stay with the cattle drive, at least until Kilmore just north of Melbourne. Sean would be paid three pounds a week and he could select and keep an older horse from his mob, and select a saddle and bridle from an old disused pile in the spare wagon. The trip would take between ten to twelve weeks.

Maluka gave Sean five shillings and pointed, "Meet me at the stockyards down there in three days from now. We'll be leaving the next day." He had pointed to several paddocks with wagons and horses. They shook hands and Sean left. There were two more people waiting to speak with Maluka.

For the next three days Sean strolled around Sydney town. There was no doubt it was a beautiful harbor. The shoreline was dotted with inlets and several small beaches. They were not as plentiful as he saw as his ship approached the entrance to the harbor but they were covered with golden sand. He could see some dark people on the beaches but they were too far away to discern.

On the second day Sean was strolling down one of Sydney's narrow streets when he came face to face with a group of Australian native Aborigines. There were five of them, virtually naked except for an animal skin draped over their shoulders. The two men had wide shoulders, slim legs and walked with a dignified air. The sole woman was small, dainty and quite shy. She kept her head down. Two small boys were with them, trotting behind the woman.

Sean presumed she was the mother. The men carried spears and had an animal skin bag over their shoulder while the woman had a bag draped from her forehead down her back. They walked past Sean, looking neither right nor left, heading towards the harbor. They were definitely different from the Cape Town native Africans.

Sean walked down the main street past several rows of shops. They supplied most necessary goods at a reasonable price, although food was expensive. The town had substantial Government sandstone buildings and everything down to hovels which were made from poles, weatherboards and bark slab roofs with no facilities whatsoever. In time it would be called a city.

The third day was a day of anticipation – a trip into the unknown for Sean. He had not enjoyed Sydney town and would be glad to leave the smells and squalor. He walked excitedly down to the stockyards.

Maluka took him to the horse paddock. "There are several aged mares past their prime but they will give you a year or so of good work. The old saddles and harnesses are in the light weight blue wagon. You said you can sew leather; here's your chance to show me. Finally, in the wagon, amongst general items, are a small anvil, a bellows, a collection of tools, clinchers, pinchers, hammers and a barrel of horse shoes and a bag of shoe nails. There are two spare wheels strapped to the wagon sides and a barrel of axle grease. Check it out and make sure that you have all you need. We avoid any towns on our track so you need to be self-sufficient. Get it right today. You won't get a second chance."

Sean could see that Maluka was indeed the boss.

Maluka had funded the cattle drive and his reputation hinged on getting as many cattle to their destination in as good condition as possible. He would be paid per head by the receiving cattlemen upon delivery. So naturally he had allowed for as many unpredictable situations as possible.

This was to be Maluka's last overland cattle drive. He was retiring to his property in the Bendigo area. He planned to sell his horses, wagons and odds and ends at an auction in Melbourne. This was the reason for giving Sean the old mare as part of his pay.

Sean went to the blue wagon and located a bridle and saddle needing only small repairs. He had souvenired some sail needles and the hand pad he had used on-board the ship, together with a ball of twine.

The older mares had been separated from the stock horses and were milling around in a separate yard. There was a sameness with all the horses; they were either a bay or brown colour. Drovers did not ride piebalds, skewbalds or greys. They believed they spooked the cattle at night. He selected and caught a docile brown mare and named her Jess. He harnessed her with the repaired bridle and saddle, walked her around to see her gait and examined her shoes, joints and teeth. Satisfied, he painted her bridle red. It made her easier to pick out in the mob.

The saddle selection had been a little more difficult, buckles and stirrup irons were mostly missing. Sean solved the problem by selecting a standard riding saddle with a good seat. He cut the stirrup irons he needed from other well used saddles. His saddle was different from the stockmen's. They had two knee pads which were needed when turning horses in small circles, whereas his saddle had none and he wouldn't need them.

Within two hours he had a good horse, saddle and bridle. After another hour he was pleased to find the farrier and blacksmith equipment provided was adequate for the journey. The wagon had several rolled sections of an old sail roped to its sides and a dinghy tied on top upside down. He packed his leather bag and swag aboard. This completed the blue wagon's load.

All around the stockyards was activity. He could see the cook and his young helper stowing their utensils and packing supplies into two lightweight red wagons. When the stockmen realised Sean was the farrier, they lined up to have their horses' shoes checked. Maluka also had all the spare horses checked. Six horses needed reshoeing. This took Sean the rest of the day.

It had been a long day. That night he slept soundly. He noticed that Maluka and several stockmen had revolvers in their belts. Others had carbines in their saddle holsters. Sean kept his revolver under his shirt in an open holster. He didn't need to let anyone know he was armed.

A rooster woke the camp. Some stockmen were already up and about having a bite to eat and a cuppa from the cook.

Maluka bellowed, "We leave in one hour." A sense of excitement was in the air. The cattle were to be collected ten miles south of Sydney. Maluka and the head stockman led the team from of town. Spectators gave them a wave, wishing them good luck. The Sydney community knew when an overland trip was heading south to Victoria.

The procession was over a hundred yards long. As well as the wagons, there were twelve stockmen and four mounted rouseabouts. Sean rode in front of the three four-wheeled wagons bringing up the rear, each pulled by two big strong hairy horses. No bullocks, they only travel at ten miles a day – too slow. The eight spare horses were tied to the tailgates of the wagons.

Maluka rode his horse with the relaxed manner of a seasoned stockman. He sat tall, with loose reins and long stirrups straps.

Sean was uncomfortable. He hadn't ridden for many months and soon became saddle sore and began to stand in his stirrups.

The head stockman saw his agitation and suggested that he ride on a wagon until he became used to the saddle. Sean quickly agreed. Maluka just smiled but said nothing. It took Sean over a week to be able to last a day in the saddle.

The Constable and the Miner

When the team arrived at the cattle holding area, Maluka went to meet the group of cattlemen standing by a sign post pointing in the direction of Melbourne. Behind them, a large mob of cattle were being herded in a circle by several stockmen.

Sean watched with interest as the head stockman arranged his men to count the cattle and check their brands and then decide on an agreed head count with the cattlemen. It was sundown when the count was finished and the signatures agreeing the transfer of twelve hundred cattle was completed between Maluka and the cattlemen.

Maluka's stockmen now took over herding the mob. The cattle were kept in a circle with the stockmen riding slowly around. Some of these stockmen were quietly singing folk songs, probably taught to them by their parents when they were children.

A fire was lit and a meal prepared.

The meal was welcome. Sean hadn't eaten since they left Sydney. The cook used to be a British Army cook and he knew how to cater and handle potentially unruly groups, such as a team of drovers. They were treated to boiled mutton and a potato followed by a rice pudding, all washed down with pannikins of tea. The meal was both filling and nourishing and they could have as much as they wished.

The camp settled down soon after eating. The men arranged their swags and bedding around the fire. There was little talk. Some lay back smoking.

Sean lay on his back with his head on the saddle looking at the stars and enjoying the folk songs. He was at peace with the world even with his saddle soreness. A harmonica lulled him to sleep.

The day started at sunrise, with the cook sounding the breakfast bell. He and his offsider had been up for an hour. The water had been boiled for tea, dampers cooked and a slab of meat ready for the men to cut slices for now and their midday meal.

The men sat quietly enjoying a bite and a cuppa. The stockmen had already fed and watered their horses and saddled them before breakfast. Their shoes had been checked last night. They were ready to travel.

At noon they would eat on horseback, a canvas water bag had been slung around the horse's neck to satisfy the stockman's thirst during the day. His hat would be filled to supply his horse with a drink of water.

Maluka had selected two rouseabouts who were experienced bushmen as forward scouts. They had both travelled with cattle drives to Victoria before. Their job was to ensure the cattle were headed to water. Whether it was a river, a creek or a billabong, it didn't matter; just so long as it had plenty of water. Another role, but of secondary importance, was finding suitable crossing places for rivers they encountered. They needed either reasonably flat country where the cattle could safely swim across, or better still, fords they could walk across.

Many other herds had travelled south before and had left a track of flattened ground growth and shrubs. Generally Maluka would follow the same course. The bushmen were the first to leave, heading south in a flurry of dust. They would be expected back by nightfall. Round the camp fire at night they would share their exploratory findings with all. Maluka would decide overnight the course for tomorrow,

The stockmen started to move the cattle from their circle formation and slowly arrange them into a long formation, the wingmen cantering backwards and forwards, gradually shaping the line.

Maluka watched as the herd moved out. The leading cattle were walking calmly, following the lead stockman, and the three wagons bringing up the rear of the mob with the spare horses in tow. The drive was starting as planned and the team was now relaxing a little. The cattle would travel fifteen to twenty miles each day.

Sean was still experiencing saddle soreness and after an hour or so joined the blue wagon on the padded seat to gain some relief from his soreness.

The driver was a young American adventurer named Ben Atkins from California. He had tried gold mining with little luck and decided to see the world. He had worked his passage to Sydney as a deck hand and decided this job was a good way to see the Colonies of Australia. Maluka gave him the job as he had driven stage coaches in America for six months. They chatted away, suffocated by the dust from the cattle. The drive was monotonous; watching the rumps of walking cattle for days was not very exciting. Sean thought, *I've got over three months of this.*

The days rolled along, travelling up hill and down dale, averaging about fifteen miles a day. They had left Sydney at the end of winter to ensure they crossed the Murray and Goulburn Rivers before the waters from the melting snows in the Alps flowed west and raised the rivers levels. The flood waters rose up to fifteen feet in some river sections.

The bushmen knew their jobs. They picked good tracks where water was available most of the time. Some minor delays occurred due to encountering a few wild aborigine warriors. Some flour and tobacco averted any confrontation. Water was only a problem once, when they travelled for two days without any but no cattle died. They were also successful locating fords at the rivers and creeks on their track. Only once did they need to swim the cattle. Fortunately only six were lost.

Crossing one river required the wagons to be floated. This was when the dinghy was used. A stockman swam his horse across the river towing a longline. The wagons were emptied and their contents pulled across the river in the dinghy. Another line was used to pull the dinghy back to be reloaded. It was time consuming, but effective.

The sails were then pulled under the wagons and the corners pulled up and over the top and tied crosswise, making a floatable box! They were pulled across the river and then reloaded. This took nearly all day.

The country they were travelling through was green and heavily treed in most parts. In the distance the snow topped alps could be seen with snow glittering in the sunlight. With the cloudless day, the scene was worthy of a famous painter putting it on canvas.

Camping by a river, Ben and Sean had a swim. Afterwards when sitting on the bank they saw a strange creature swimming in shallow water. It had a duckbill, short furry webbed feet, with dangerous looking spurs on its back legs and had a body like a beaver. When they described the animal around the campfire that night, two other stockmen nodded and said it was called a platypus and it was the weirdest animal in the world, made from several different animals. Sean agreed; it was an unusual animal.

The unique Australian wildlife was everywhere, particularly birds of all colours and sizes, many with unusual sounds such as the laughing jackass or kookaburra. Large flocks of black or white parrots were common, as were the galahs, another parrot, coloured grey and pink. Snakes were common and were to be avoided; many were deadly.

Koalas inhabited eucalyptus trees. They were short – one to two feet long – and tubby with long sharp claws, large eyes and a button nose. Another unusual animal was the tubby wombat. It lived in an underground burrow. All types of lizards were common in the bush with the goanna being over three feet long.

Apart from daily inspecting the wagon wheels, harnesses and seeing if the stockmen were happy with their horses, Sean had little to do. Once a week he greased the wagon axles. He often sat with Ben and chatted. They discussed their lives and hopes for the future. Ben said he would like to travel to the Bendigo goldfields when the cattle drive was completed. With his experience in California, he was optimistic he would be successful. A gold miner needed to be an optimist. Sean was still unsure of his plans.

Sean's first challenge came when he found a wagon wheel hub had split. Unless it was repaired it would soon collapse. It would not last the trip. That night, together with several helpers, he swapped the wheel with one of the spares. During the night stops over the next week, Sean started to repair the hub. First he hammered a strap of hoop iron into a circle to fit over the outside of the split hub, after having shaved the outside of the hub flat. He intended to fuse the two ends of the now circular iron strap and hammer it over the flat section of the hub. The cook gave Sean a small bag of coal which he fired up in a small brazier by pumping the bellows at the heated coal until the ends of the hoop were red hot. He then hammered the metal ends together on the anvil, in a flurry of impressive sparks.

He left the hoop to cool. If it was not fully circular it would be easier to shape when cooled slowly. The next afternoon he offered up the hoop to the hub. He was happy, it was slightly smaller. Sean then tied a section of wire around the hub and tightened it until the wood split had been pulled closed.

The moment of truth had arrived – could the hoop be hammered over the flat section of the hub? Within ten minutes the hoop had been belted into position. Sean untied the wire and the split remained tightly closed, held by the metal hoop.

Maluka had been watching his efforts and smiled. "Yes, you know your trade." He rode away.

Maluka was seated on his horse at the top of the river bank watching the last wagon leaving the water. He was satisfied with the success of the crossing, even though the water was only three to four feet deep it was still possible to lose a few head of cattle. None had been lost today. The stockman who had been riding alongside the wagon suddenly stopped and dismounted.

He just stood there looking at his horse. Maluka could see the horse had its off side front leg bent awkwardly. The stockman removed his bridle and saddle and walked towards him, his head was down.

He stopped in front of Maluka and quietly said, "He stepped in a hole. His leg's broken."

Maluka nodded, drew his revolver and offered it to the stockman who shook his head and walked to the nearest wagon, selected another horse, harnessed it and rode after the herd. He did not look back.

The head stockman had just ridden up and had seen the incident. He took the revolver from Maluka and rode down to the river to the injured horse. He dismounted, sat on his heels, rolled a cigarette and waited for the last wagon to disappear in the distance. Stockmen became very attached to their horses, they were friends and had a strong bond and to lose one was a very emotional event. It was understandable the reluctance of the rider to end his horse's life.

The cattle drive had vanished into the distance, only a dust cloud was visible. The head stockman grasped the horse's mane and led it hobbling into the river. After the gunshot, the horse collapsed immediately into the slow flowing water and floated downstream.

The head stockman watched for a while, mounted his horse, cantered after the herd and handed Maluka his revolver. Around the campfire that night not a word was said about the incident. They left the stockman with his thoughts.

Sean often rode with the stockmen as they trotted up and down the long trail of cattle, keeping them within the herd. He enjoyed watching their riding skills when they chased cattle who managed to wander away.

The horses turned in their own length, when reeled around by their rider. No matter which way the cattle turned, the horse would be in front, blocking their path, with the stockman cracking his whip. Rarely did he strike the animal but if he did the animal would remember the sting of the whip. Within ten minutes or so the cattle would be trotting back to the main mob.

Sean once saw a stockman cut the head off a snake with one accurate crack of his whip. Such was the skill of the Australian stockmen.

Monotonous as the cattle drive was, Sean was bored at times but never depressed.

Each week the scenery changed. They had started in a very green and hilly environment, but as the weeks rolled by, the land became flatter and the previous verdant green changed to a lighter green as the weather decidedly grew warmer.

At times he would ride away from the drive to do some exploring on his own, although he always kept the cattle in sight. He would see the ever present kangaroos, emus and sometimes dingos, a small red native dog which was a prolific killer of lambs. The wedge tailed eagle was also capable of carrying off small lambs.

The quietness and isolation of the Australian bush gave Sean a serenity which he had not felt before. The sounds of the native birds such as the warble of the magpies and the quark of the crows completed Sean's peaceful feeling.

After a few hours of meandering he would return to the drive. He did these short trips many times. Maluka said nothing.

As summer approached, storm clouds often formed, then vanished. However it was inevitable that one day a storm cloud would bring rain. It was a typical early summer storm, very dark skies, short bursts of heavy rain together with the dread of all stockmen – lightning.

Sean was on the crease of a hill. A small part of the herd had moved quicker than the bulk of the cattle and was on the other side of the crest of a steep hill.

A lightning strike, followed by a thunder clap, hit and split a large dry tree with a loud crack. The crack panicked the small forward herd of about one hundred cattle and they stampeded. The three stockmen immediately headed for the front of the cattle. Their arms low with the bridle and their feet forward in their stirrups, they galloped hard. Initially the cattle continued off their track but suddenly they began turning. Riding hard, one stockman headed to intercept the leaders, cracking his whip again and again. A second stockman followed about ten yards behind him, cracking his whip vigorously. The leaders soon began tiring and turned away from the riders and back onto their original track.

The cattle soon slowed down to a walk and began bawling noisily. The stockmen kept them walking slowly until the main herd caught up an hour or so later. Surprisingly the main herd had not changed their pace. The hill must have muffled the loud noise crack made by the tree when it was split by the lightning.

Sean rode after the stockmen to watch the action. The memory of the dramatic event would remain with him for many years.

That night around the camp fire Maluka just said, "You men did a good job today. I watched from the hill. I knew you could handle the stampede."

The bushmen had been exploring along the mighty Murray River for a safe crossing.

They reported that they had located a wide ford with virtually no water flowing. They had beaten the flood waters, or so they thought.

The day they arrived at the ford, two riders galloped up to Maluka and advised that the river had started to rise. "You had better move your cattle across quickly. The water can rise ten feet in a matter of hours. We're farming nearby and we've seen it happen."

Maluka thanked them and quickly alerted the stockmen who raced alongside the herd cracking their whips and shouting. They soon got the cattle lumbering along and quickly heading to the river crossing. He told the wagon drivers to move forward and cross the river with the cattle and not to wait at the rear as they normally did.

When the wagons reached the river, the waters were already starting to rise and the flow had become stronger. The drivers headed their horses into the water urging the cattle on with quick flicks of the reins.

By the time they reached the other bank the water was already up to the wagons' axles. The first half of the cattle was still able to wade, although the water was almost over their rumps. The local riders were right, the waters were rising rapidly and the flow increasing.

The remaining cattle had to swim in the fast moving water. However the last fifty or so were swept downstream, together with a stockman who had slipped off his swimming horse and was hanging onto its tail. A mile down the river there was a sharp bend blocked by a large fallen tree. Over the years, debris had collected in it and this had helped form a sandbank.

The stockman and most of the cattle reached the sandbank and quickly climbed to safety. Unfortunately a dozen or so cattle were swept further downstream by the fast flowing water and disappeared from sight.

The stockman mounted his horse and gradually herded the surviving cattle into a small mob. They were easy to handle as they were tired after their ordeal. The track back to the main herd was difficult. Dodging trees and scrubs slowed their progress and it was dark when they re-joined the camp.

Maluka was in the process of sending out a search party to look for the stockman when he arrived. The stockman had his shirt ripped in several places, his arms were bleeding and he had a cut cheek. Such was the brittleness of the tree branches. After washing the wounds with hot water, axle grease was liberally and successfully applied. No infection developed.

Considering they had only lost a dozen cattle out of a herd of nearly twelve hundred, they all felt they had done a good job and, most importantly, they had beaten the alpine snow flood waters.

The remaining river and creek crossings in Victoria were not subject to the rapid floods like the Murray River experienced and these few were crossed with no loss of cattle. The stockmen had become expert at handling the swimming or fording of the cattle across water courses.

The land south of the Murray River was very challenging and slowed the drive. The land was reasonably flat but heavily treed.

It was difficult to keep the cattle bunched in such country. Some stockmen and, sometimes their horses, suffered cuts from the low branches of trees. Axle grease was again applied liberally to keep the flies off the open cuts on both stockmen and animals.

The bushmen were still following the tracks made by the previous cattle drives, even in places where the track was nearly overgrown.

They were nearing the end of their long journey. Most of the cattle would be sold to a broker in Kilmore for distribution throughout the Victorian eastern highlands. The remaining four hundred would be taken to the Melbourne sale yards and be auctioned together with Maluka's horses, wagons and equipment. He would then pay off the remaining droving team and retire to his property.

Sean and Ben had become firm friends and, during their chats on his wagon, they had decided to leave when they reached Kilmore and travel to the Bendigo goldfields. Sean had underground coal mining experience and Ben had gold mining experience above ground. Possibly their skills would complement each other.

Ben told Sean he had made a deal with Maluka to obtain two of the other older horses together with some shovels and picks, one horse to ride and the other to be used as a pack horse.

They reached the outskirts of Kilmore on a very hot, dry and dusty day. Maluka and the head stockmen headed into town to meet with the broker. The next morning the broker and several other stockmen rode to the herd and started to separate the broker's cattle.

Maluka addressed his men and, after paying those who were leaving, thanked them for their efforts, and wished them good luck and fortune.

Sean and Ben went to him, and shook his hand. "Thank you for the experience." They mounted their horses, gave a few waves and headed into town. They did not look back. They were looking forward. To what?

CHAPTER SIX

The Gold Adventure

Sean and Ben stopped at the first inn they came to and enjoyed their first ale at three pence a glass and a sit down meal of eggs, vegetables and chicken stew for a shilling.

The bar was crowded with shearers who were 'Lambing down'. They had passed their cheques over the bar to the innkeeper. When they had spent (drank) their money, he would tell them to move on.

Many were drunk and it was inevitable that a dispute would occur. The yelling and shouting soon escalated into punches. Most missed their target. One drunk was struck heavily on the jaw and staggered towards their table, spilling Sean's ale. He stood up and picked up the drunk and hurled him back into the melee. The innkeeper pushed the fighting group out onto the street where they gradually tired and either sat down or fell down on the road.

Sean and Ben had decided to ride to the Heathcote gold mines first to try their luck. On the way there, during a tea break, two horsemen joined them for a brew. They had been mining in the Heathcote area for a few months for limited reward. There was gold in the area but only a few miners had been successful in finding it. They had given up and were headed south to Melbourne. Sean and Ben decided to give it a try for a few months and if they were unsuccessful they would move on.

The ride to Heathcote was through dense forest and hilly all the way. It took them nearly two days and another day to locate a suitable place.

There were several miners working in the area and few appreciated newcomers.

One of the miners walked over to them. "Are you intending to stay or just riding through?"

Ben shrugged his shoulders. "Just looking. Why do you ask?"

The stranger answered, "Well I'm willing to let you have two mine sites for a few pounds. It's got potential. I've made some money. My mother is ill and I'm heading home. I was mining it with my father."

"We could be interested. Show us the mine," Ben answered.

The mine sites were on the slope of a creek and the mine about twenty feet deep.

Ben could see that the soil and rocks were similar to that of the Californian goldfields. "How much do you want?" he asked.

"How about twenty pounds?"

Ben shook his head. "Make it ten pounds and we have a deal."

They shook hands and each handed over five pounds from their cattle drive pay. Sean and Ben were now goldminers.

The Constable and the Miner

They named the mine El Dorado. They wasted no time in setting up camp. They needed to buy canvas for beds, a few cooking utensils and some food. There was a small tent.

The mine had a windlass for hauling up buckets with rocks from the mine and some hammers, shovels and picks. The cradle had horizontal grooves over which extracted soil was washed down while the cradle was tilted and rocked. There was a grass area alongside the top of the mine site. They hobbled the horses there after putting them on a long line.

All miners were required to carry a valid licence or be fined or detained.

Ben rode into Heathcote the next day to obtain miner's licenses for Sean and himself to work the claims. It now cost twenty shillings per year. The previous year the Victorian Government had been charging a miner's license fee of thirty shillings per month when squatters were only paying ten pounds per year, an exorbitant and unfair licence fee for the miners.

The licence was also used as an identification card. It detailed his beard colour, his visible tattoos, eye colour, physical disabilities etc. The police, or 'Joes', licence inspections were virtually 'diggers hunts', often conducted with violence. Many unsuccessful miners could not afford to pay the fee and would hide in mine shafts or hide in the bush. It was inevitable that the Ballaarat miners would revolt and the Eureka Stockade Rebellion occurred to the shame of the Victorian Government.

Ben did the necessary buying. Basically they lived

on mutton, damper some vegetables and copious cups of tea. Meanwhile Sean chopped down some small trees to be used as frames to make their bunks, table and seats.

That night they sat down and agreed on some ground rules.

1. Only one person would be in the mine at any time.
2. The other would work the windlass and bring water from the creek.
3. They would do equal time in the mine.
4. Ben would decide if the mine was viable.
5. Any gold found would be kept in the mine.
6. Any gold found would be assayed in Melbourne, to avoid a middle man.
7. They would always wear an obvious leather pouch around their neck.
8. They would have minimum communication with other miners.
9. The three horses would be tied alongside the tent at night.

The mine had foot notches on the inside walls, together with beams supporting the walls to a depth of ten feet. The next ten feet was mainly rock and unsupported. The previous owner had started to burrow to the side where there were traces of white quartz. Ben was in two minds – to continue down or across?

They soon got into a routine and Sean slowly learnt to identify rocks worth hammering into smaller pieces and worth washing in the puddling tub.

After washing the crushed rock pieces, they were poured through a sieve into the cradle. Water was then poured onto the cradle and it was rocked from side to side.

He would closely watch what was not being washed away. Any obvious gold nuggets would be removed immediately to assist in flushing the rubbish. After the soil, shale rock and other debris was washed away, gold being heavier, would remain in the grooves of the corrugated sheet, be it specks, alluvial or gold nuggets. The remains in the sieve were also checked, hopefully for larger nuggets.

The water for the puddling tub and the cradle was collected from the creek by a bucket tied to a rope. The place where the water was collected was about ten feet on the upstream side of a large rock which slowed the water flow. The mine was yielding some gold and quartz but the quantity was not very profitable. They had been at it for four weeks and were losing confidence.

Ben called Sean to come up. It was too early to swap over jobs. Sean was curious.

Ben was excited. "Where did you get the last bucket of water? The mud in the bottom had gold in it."

Sean said, "I moved closer to the rock as the track had become slippery. I'll go and get some more now." He grabbed a bucket and walked to the creek and dropped the bucket in the same spot as before. He made sure that he dragged it along the creek bed. Excitedly he walked back to Ben and gave him the bucket and then went down the mine shaft to continue working. An hour or so later he climbed up for lunch. Ben was sitting quietly, sipping a cup of tea.

He said very calmly, "We have found good gold. The creek soil is loaded with it. That rock has probably been a natural trap for hundreds of years. I suggest that we continue as normal until we can't find any more alluvial gold in that particular spot." Sean nodded agreement.

For the next few days each bucket yielded alluvial gold. After five days the gold stopped. They had cleaned out the pocket of alluvial. Should they go or stay?

The suggestion of wearing Ben's pouches paid off a few days later. The week after he had placed a few grains of gold in their neck pouches, they were robbed. They were eating lunch when a horseman rode up, and pulled out his pistol. "Give me your neck pouches quickly or I will shoot you."

They had no choice. As soon as they handed them over, he rode off. Later when the thief checked the pouches he would assume that they were just another team of miners battling to find a strike. Ben had learnt the pouch trick in California.

The weather had been warm but rain was expected. The first heavy storm lasted for twenty four hours and started to flow into the mine. They dug trenches around the mine to divert the rain water from flowing into it and laid two cross poles over the mine entry and covered it with a canvas sheet. The creek became swollen with fallen trees and other debris. The rock below their mine site had trapped a large tree. It was two days before the water stopped flowing but the tree remained and blocked the water flow down to the other miners.

Three miners approached their camp and asked if Sean and Ben could help remove the tree. They had explosives for mining but were unsure how to use them on the tree. Ben agreed to explode the tree. He had the miners drill three inch holes equidistant along the trunk. They moved back to a safe distance near their mines. The explosion was spectacular, the tree literally blew apart. Only small branches were left to float down the creek.

Sean and Ben went down to the rock where they collected their water and found the rock had been completely shattered. Sean watched as the water subsided but Ben was standing in the water picking up pieces of rock, throwing most back into the creek. He kept six, gave three to Sean and kept three for himself. "Put them in your pocket and let's get back to the camp."

They went into the tent, placed them on the table and sat looking at them. Even Sean could see they looked like gold nuggets. They were! They now had some quartz gold from the mine, alluvial gold from the creek and six nuggets. What should they do – stay or go? The mine had not been very successful but the alluvial gold was valuable and the nuggets very valuable.

The previous week Ben had been in Heathcote for supplies and had heard a Gold Escort would be coming through en route to Melbourne from Bendigo, the day after tomorrow. Many travellers joined the escort for safety.

Sean and Ben decided that they had been fortunate enough with their gamble and felt they should now enjoy the benefits of their efforts. They had pounds of gold not ounces. If there were any more gold nuggets in the creek, they could wait.

Early on the morning of the Gold Escort's transiting, they quietly gathered the belongings they felt they should take, packed the gold into each saddle bag, fed, watered the horses and patiently waited by the road, ready to join the cavalcade to Melbourne. They left one horse with food and water for three days. They gave no indication to the other miners they would be away for a few days, in case they thought the mine site was abandoned.

The clinking of horse harnesses signalled the coming of the Escort up the hill from Heathcote. The officer in charge nodded to them but said nothing. In the past he had seen many riders and wagons join his troop. The Escort would only stop at planned stops – overnight and midday, a break for the men and the horses.

At the overnight stop at Wallan, Sean and Ben slept with the two saddle bags under their waists with the buckles facing down. Sean still had his revolver in his sovereigns belt. The Escort kept a steady pace of eight miles per hour. The next day they were in Melbourne and immediately went to the Government Assayer's office.

The clerk who received their gold was impressed with the six nuggets and was curious as to where they had been found but didn't press them for an answer. No doubt he had seen many other good sized nuggets. He told them to return next day for the evaluation results.

After obtaining a receipt for the deposit of their gold, they left the horses at a stable near the assayer's office and went to a nearby hotel for a meal and a bed. Early next morning they strolled through the streets of Melbourne. It was not like London or California but it was growing. It was disappointing.

The roads were being gravelled and the river was having wharves built. The buildings' standards varied from impressive, good, bad to indifferent and were made from bluestone rock, wooden planks or bark slabs.

After the fresh air of the countryside, Melbourne smelt of human, animal and vegetation waste and the river was not very clean either.

They were both excited. Ben thought the gold was valuable; Sean was optimistic. After a quick breakfast and a short walk to the assayer's office, they presented themselves for the report. When they announced who they were, they were ushered into a side office.

A tall distinguished man entered and introduced himself as the Government Assayer.

"Well, gentlemen, I have good news for you. The six

nuggets and the alluvial gold were of exceptional high quality. Even the quartz gold was of reasonable quality."

He smiled. "We have valued all of your gold at six hundred pounds."

Sean could not believe the figure. Ben was speechless.

Sean managed to splutter, "Thank you very much."

They looked at each other, shook hands vigorously and patted each other on the back. Three hundred pounds each; it was a small fortune to them.

The assayer offered them a cup of tea and sat with them. He wished to know where they had located the gold. It was a requirement to advise the Government of the area for demographic purposes. The exact site was not needed. Ben gave a rough area of within a one mile circle. This satisfied the assayer.

The Assayer's Office and the Bank of Australasia were next to each other and the gold-to-money transaction was easily accomplished. Sean deposited his entire share in the bank. He had sovereigns in his belt. He didn't need the money – yet.

That night the two sat together and talked of their future. Ben wanted to continue mining. They still had the miner's right for the Heathcote mine but Sean wanted another life. He'd had enough of the loneliness of droving and mining and was now moderately wealthy. He wanted a normal communal life. Finally, they agreed to keep the mine; Ben would continue to mine it.

They were in no hurry and stopped at several villages on their way back to Kilmore, enjoying the views towards Melbourne and Port Phillip Bay from the mountain range. Ben was to continue on to Heathcote.

The two friends sat down for a farewell lunch. They had been a good team, hardly an angry word crossed between them but it was time for a change and they both realised it.

They agreed to keep in contact via the local Cobb and Co. office, the stage coach operators. Sean would use the Heathcote office to keep Ben informed of his location. The farewell was quick, a hand shake and a pat on the back and they parted ways. Sean had mixed feelings as he watched Ben ride down the street heading north as he headed west to Kyneton. Would they ever meet again?

Sean soon arrived in Kyneton, an impressive farming centre on the Campaspe River. Riding down the main street, looking at the shops and commercial buildings, Sean saw a painted sign advertising for a blacksmith.

This could be what he was looking for – a job of his calling. To his delight he got the job. He could start today if he wanted to. So soon!

Sean agreed to start work with the farrier as soon as he found accommodation and a stable. The farrier suggested he stay at the Royal Hotel until he had settled in the town. He also said he had a spare stable at the rear of the business, for Jess. Problem solved. Sean started work the next day. He was no longer a miner. He could not believe his good fortune.

CHAPTER SEVEN

Bush Bound

The day of John's departure for Kyneton was a sad day for the family. Except for a few days, they had not been apart for any long periods. The women had tears in their eyes and George stood quietly behind them. John sensibly made the farewell quick and headed down the street, leading his pack horse. He turned and waved as he rounded the corner and then headed north.

John left Melbourne mid-morning for Keilor. He alternately cantered and trotted the horses for half an hour, then walked them for fifteen minutes. He continued this pace until he reached Essendon where he stopped for a quick meal, after feeding and watering the horses.

The ride to Keilor was leisurely. The road side now had more buildings and he enjoyed seeing the green rolling hills with wisps of smoke from the distant farm houses.

He wondered where the farmers had come from. He presumed that some had fled Ireland because of the potato famine and the British subjugation.

Others had probably left the harsh English weather, seeking a new life for themselves and their families. He stopped a few times and had a chat with other passing riders.

He was also aware of the many walkers heading to the goldfields. Some were pushing carts, and others pushed wheel barrows loaded with their daily essentials, together with picks and spades. Each miner quietly plodded along with optimism and determination showing on their face.

He stopped at the top of the hill overlooking Keilor. It was typical of many Victorian villages – an inn, several shops, a smithy, a police lock up with horses and gigs tied up outside the various shops – a pretty scene. It nestled in a small valley alongside a tranquil river.

He walked the horses down the hill to the local constabulary. He was welcomed by the local sergeant who introduced him to two civilians he was meeting, one who was the innkeeper. When the innkeeper realised John was one of the three policemen who had captured the escapees, he offered him free accommodation.

That night John slept better than his previous visit when he had to sleep in the police stable. The hospitality was gratefully received. Hospitality was not so forthcoming in Melbourne.

John departed at sun up and made such good time to Gisborne he decided to continue on to Woodend. The Woodend road was notorious for bushranger activity and John had been warned not to travel alone. He spotted two carts heading north from Gisborne and approached them, asking if they minded if he joined them. They were delighted to have an armed police officer in their party, as they also were concerned about travelling through the Woodend Black Forrest.

The road snaked down a long hill through a dense

forest with little sunlight shining through. The travellers remained alert for the entire three mile trip; each man hand his hand close to his gun. Fortunately they did not encounter any bushrangers. John could understand the travellers' apprehension. It was the most forbidding place he had been in and that included the streets of London's East Docks.

As it was late afternoon, John decided to remain overnight in Woodend. One of the travellers, Edward Sims, had a brother-in-law who lived in a large house in the village and he offered John a bed for the night, which he gladly accepted.

John reciprocated their hospitality and took them to an inn for dinner. After feeding and watering the horses, he retired to a comfortable bed and enjoyed a good night's sleep. He was now beginning to experience real country hospitality.

The final stage of his trip started early. After a hearty breakfast, compliments of Edward and his brother-in-law, John headed for Kyneton. The road had few bends and only a gentle incline. The goldfield walkers were still on the road, on and on ever onwards, in hope.

John started to count them for something to do but eventually got bored and lost interest and started counting the different birds. He was surprised at the numbers he saw. The countryside now had a sameness about it. He had seen enough green paddocks, livestock and forests. All he wanted now was to reach his destination.

He crossed a small river and trotted up the main street. The town was bigger than he expected. It was late morning and bustling with people, horses and gigs outside shops. He asked a passer-by for the directions to the police barracks and soon located it. He sat on his horse looking at the bluestone building.

Actually there were two buildings. They were small but impressive. After tying up his horses he entered the building and introduced himself to the duty constable who led him to an office and directed him to enter. Behind a desk was District Inspector Brittan. He looked up and smiled. "Sergeant Williams I presume."

John took an immediate liking to District Inspector Brittan. He was as tall as John and had a solid build. He had a determined expression behind his disarming smile.

Brittan motioned John to be seated as he opened his transfer documents. With a few 'ums' and 'ahs' he flicked through the pages, quickly reading them.

He looked up. "Well, you certainly made your mark at the Melbourne Barracks. You will definitely be an asset here. You may not know, but my sub inspector is on extended leave with a broken leg. His leg hit a fence when he was chasing a thief and his horse fell. Your experience will help cover his duties. You will find a wide variety of challenges up here. Many require a personal touch and, as a family man, you will be well suited. After I introduce you to our team, I'll help you to arrange your accommodation."

The Kyneton Constabulary consisted of an inspector, a sub inspector, a sergeant and four constables. After the introductions the Inspector mentioned that the position of sub inspector and sergeant would eventually be combined, but he didn't know when. He was unsure if the current sub inspector would be returning to duty in Kyneton.

Accommodation was soon organised at the Royal Hotel. The hotel was only a short ride from the barracks and he was shown a comfortable room and advised the hotel served good meals. He was given two days leave to acquaint himself with the town, its buildings and shops. He was sure Jane would enjoy living here. It appeared to be a friendly and clean town, which would be a change from the Melbourne bustle and squalor.

On his first day on duty, the Inspector walked John around Kyneton and introduced him to the people of note and the leading shop owners. They all welcome him and offered him any help he may need.

John happened to mention that he was looking for married accommodation as he had a wife and two children in Melbourne.

The Mayor nodded. "Come and see me in a week's time. I'll be in Melbourne until then but I may be able to help resolve your accommodation problem." John acknowledged the offer and made a mental note to see him.

John soon settled into his new environment. There was more horse riding required than he had expected but he soon got over his saddle soreness. The country air was a delight. Even the police horse yard and stables smelt cleaner. The barracks had a large stable with stalls for eight horses, with another six horses rotated from the horse yard. He placed his two horses with them.

The town was much quieter than Melbourne. The hotels were much easier to monitor. The main difference was that the crimes here related mostly to rural situations – livestock stealing, forged brands and water rights.

The Inspector was correct when he said that a personal touch was needed in the country. A policeman might know a few of the community but all the community would know the policeman and how he handled a crime. Within a few days, John's skills would be tested when he went to investigate a stolen sheep complaint.

Two farmers shared the responsibility to keep their dividing fence in good condition. George Keane's farmhouse was in the corner of his property and within fifty yards of the dividing fence. James Dunne's farmhouse was in the far corner of his property and about a mile from Keane's. Their land had steep hills and several dense pockets of trees. Dunne had just started shearing and discovered his two prize rams were missing and had reported the theft.

John and a constable, who knew the district, went to meet with Dunne.

John found him busy shearing his flock of three hundred sheep.

"Have you double checked the number of your rams?" asked John, wanting to make sure there really was a crime to investigate.

Dunne angrily answered, "Yes, do you think I'm an idiot? Go and do your job."

The constable suggested that they ride around the fences. John nodded in agreement and they rode away from the shearing shed.

The fence was intact for nearly half a mile until they reached a corner between the properties where they found a small opening. A pole had split and a rail had dropped to the ground. The constable didn't think it was big enough for any sheep to get through let alone a ram.

They rode back to Dunne and told him of their discovery.

He immediately flew into a rage. "That bloody Irishman. I'll kill him for stealing my rams."

"When did you last check your fences?" asked John calmly.

Ignoring the question, Dunne demanded, "Go and arrest him." He then went back to the shearing shed.

John and the constable rode to George Keane's farmhouse. He saw them coming and waved a hello. He invited them into the house for tea.

When John explained his visit, George just laughed. "I know of the hole and a ram would not be able to get through it. If *he* got off his arse he would find his two rams over there."

He pointed to a thick clump of trees in the corner of the paddock on Dunne's property. The two missing rams were standing resting in the shade.

John laughed, guessing at how Dunne would accept this result.

It appeared that both George and Dunne had wanted the property that George had eventually purchased and now farmed. Dunne still resented George's ownership.

James Dunne was standing with a group of shearers when he saw them coming. He stood with his feet apart and his hands on his hips.

John dismounted and handed the reins to the constable. He walked to within three feet of Dunne.

"Well?" said Dunne.

John unsmiling replied, "Yes, we have found your rams."

"Good, have you arrested him?"

"No, but I'm thinking of arresting you for wasting police time," John replied.

Dunne's attitude changed from one of aggression to one of shock.

John continued. "You have wasted a day of police time having us come out here to investigate a false report. Your rams are in the top corner of your property in a stand of trees opposite your neighbour's farmhouse." Several of the shearers started laughing. John turned his back to Dunne, mounted his horse and they rode back to town. He left Dunne wondering and worrying if he would be charged.

The story was around the district the next day. The next afternoon, as John was writing his report, the inspector walked in.

"You seem to have had an interesting day yesterday. It's all around town how you handled Dunne. He has a reputation of a bully. Will you charge him?"

John shook his head. "No, I think he's been embarrassed enough."

The Inspector nodded and returned to his office.

The following week John visited the Mayor's office to make an appointment, which was unnecessary as the Mayor saw him enter the building and invited him into his office. William Miles had been born in Hobart and came to Kyneton with his parents to farm in the district. He had been mayor for two years and had implemented many improvements, particularly with roads and bridges. His parents had left him an eighty acre farm with a small bluestone cottage and stable.

He now lived in town with his family and had a grain store business. He had leased the acreage, except for two acres surrounding the vacant cottage. They agreed that they would meet the next day and ride to the farm.

The day dawned, sunny with very little cloud. It would be a pleasant ride. John met William outside the mayoral office and, after their greetings they headed north out of town. The road had a few turns and was in reasonable condition. During the half hour ride they spoke of their families.

William's children were still at school and his wife was a very keen gardener who sold her blooms at the Kyneton monthly market. She was also involved in community activities.

John suggested that their wives meet; perhaps Jane might like to become involved in the community.

William nodded.

At the top of a low hill he stopped and pointed to a small cottage with a separate stable, sited in a group of trees about a quarter of a mile away. John was impressed by the scene.

He could see that the cottage was small and overlooked some large paddocks alongside a narrow river, about one hundred yards from the farm. It reminded him of similar views in his home town, in England.

They entrance to the property was via a long narrow track leading to a picket fence gate. After tying the reins to a hitching rail outside the fence, they walked to the front door of the cottage.

John noticed that the door was made of solid wood and had a six inch diamond cut out in the middle. The door opened directly into the main room which served as a parlour and dining-kitchen area with a stove at one end.

William had purchased two at a shop sale last year. The other was in his home. Country stoves were bigger than city ones and normally had a fire burning all year round for cooking. In winter the fire door was left open for heating. Two internal doors led to two bedrooms. The larger bedroom had a small bath in one corner behind a false wall.

John could see that each of the windows also had solid wooden internal shutters with a diamond cut out at eye level.

William saw him looking at them and he commented that the solid shutters and main door were made originally for protection from aborigine attacks, but these no longer occurred and the shutters were now protection against possible bushrangers. Although none had been reported in the district and the possibility was remote, one never knew.

The cottage bluestone walls and the planked roof were in good condition and the inside walls whitewashed. The floors were smooth. They had been made with a mixture of clay and blue stone dust. The ceiling was a ship's canvas sail nailed to cross beams and was also whitewashed.

The furniture was made from oiled timber and consisted of a few beds, side tables, a wardrobe, a kitchen table with four chairs and an aged chaise lounge. A few cooking pots and pans were in a wall cupboard together with some plates, cups and cutlery. The kitchen table had a large iron teapot and several candle stick holders on it. It would be a good start.

They strolled to the stables. It was built of bluestone rock blocks and had three horse stalls and a large storage area for fodder and two carts. A small gig was in the corner covered in dust and hay.

The building was sturdy and served its purpose. The cottage and stable were in a picket fenced area of one acre. The other acre, behind the stables was for livestock and was surrounded by a four rail fence with a slip rail gate. John thought, *Perhaps we could grow vegetables on the cottage acre. The soil looks good. But water!* The cottage was on a small hill.

He asked, "Where did your water come from when you lived here?"

"We started to dig a well but didn't get around to finishing it." He pointed to a clump of bushes next to the house, where an old ship's water tank was sitting high off the ground, with a drain pipe and a collection of other pipes from the eaves. "The pipes collect the runoff from the roof planks and if you run low, you have the river. Although it's a long walk carrying a bucket. There were four of us and we rarely had to use river water. By the way the privy or dunny as we colonials call it, is behind the stable."

William explained there was a retired sea captain on the next farm. When William saw that he had nailed a sail inside his ceiling to keep out the rain and had installed a ship's water tank for house water, he paid the sea captain to purchase an old sail and a tank for him.

"I have leased the land outside the picket fence of the cottage and its livestock paddock fence. The leasee runs two hundred sheep and won't disturb you. The entire property has a four rail fence around it, to keep the sheep in. Hawthorn hedges grow alongside the rail fence, almost as a second fence.

"We have no use for the cottage but we don't want it to go to rack and ruin. You and your wife can have it on the condition you carry out any maintenance that the cottage, stables and the fencing may need and to pay any council rates due. We can both be winners."

John did not need to think. He shook Williams' hand, and smiled. "Agreed. I'm happy to sign a contract, if you so wish." They mounted their horses and rode back to town. They trusted each other and were instant friends.

That night John wrote to Jane and told her of the cottage and asked when she wanted to come to Kyneton. She replied she needed to be satisfied that the children would be able to care for themselves and then she would come to him.

The next weekend John moved into the cottage. He borrowed a cart and went shopping to bring up two lots of bedding and to stock the larder. First he swept the cottage floor and dusted the furniture. Then he polished the furniture with saddle soap and was pleasantly surprised how smart the furniture looked after two hours work. He then set up the two beds. Feeling satisfied with his effort he went for a stroll round the two acres.

The picket fence was in good condition, as was the stable. The only work required he could see were the three horse stalls; their rails were loose. The attaching bolts only needing tightening due to wood shrinkage. He decided to name the cottage, 'Woodlea'. It was the name of his mother's childhood family home.

For the next few weeks police demands were light – a few drunks, a brawl or two, a break-in, a robbery at the grocery store and a runaway gig which knocked over a senior citizen. The cells only had two prisoners, who were alleged offenders in a 'bail up' robbery and were to be taken to Melbourne for trial.

He received a letter from Jane agreeing to come to Kyneton. She would explain the situation regarding the children when they met. John had written a memo requesting leave to go to Melbourne to arrange her travel to Kyneton.

Before he had the opportunity to hand the letter to the Inspector, he was called into his office. "There is an armed Bendigo Gold Escort leaving from here tomorrow and I want you to take our prisoners to Melbourne with them. Our prisoner wagon is at the cartwright's.

"It had a cracked wheel hub and required a wheel rebuild. I've sent a constable to collect it. It should be ready for tomorrow's trip. You will have two constables, one as a coachman and one riding with you. You will have our two prisoners and you will collect two more in Woodend. Make sure that you remain alert."

He smiled. "As tomorrow is Friday, you may as well stay in Melbourne the weekend to see your family and return on Monday. Have a good trip." They shook hands and John left smiling. *Well, this assignment is a stroke of good luck,* he thought. He would be seeing Jane and his family at the weekend.

The wagon was outside the barracks when he

arrived the next morning. The constable reported the two wagon horses had been fed, watered and their harnesses checked. John instructed the constables to double check their weapons, then to handcuff the prisoners and load them into the wagon.

They were ready to join the gold escort precisely at eight a.m., when they arrived at the barracks. Their entourage consisted of a two-horse cart with two extra horses tied to the rear panel, a lieutenant, a corporal and four troopers.

The guard was well armed. Each had a pistol, a sword and a carbine in their saddle holsters. John's team each had a revolver and a shotgun.

The lieutenant shook hands with John and introduced himself as Frederick Green of the Bendigo Lancers. "We are ready to go and I can see that you are too. I suggest that you follow us at about fifty yards distance. We will stop at Woodend for an hour and have a meal break and tend the horses. We can talk more then."

John nodded and signalled his constables to mount and ride out.

The wind was cold, the sky overcast and threatening to rain. It was going to be a miserable trip. Melbourne was about sixty miles south east of Kyneton and mainly downhill. The trip would be easy for the horses but unpleasant for the police and the Lancers.

John could not help but notice how the Lancers were positioned. The corporal rode a hundred yards in front of the cart and its trooper driver. Two other troopers rode on opposite sides of the road, fifty yards in front of the cart. The next two troopers rode fifty yards behind the cart, again on opposite sides of the road with the lieutenant riding slightly behind them. John could see the logic of spreading his team.

An effective ambush would be difficult to carry out on troopers spread out over a distance of a hundred or so yards. Obviously Lieutenant Green was an experienced officer.

John and his other constable had been riding either side of the wagon. He decided to move to the rear of the wagon back about thirty yards and to the side of the road and positioned his constable back and on his opposite side.

The group had a quick trip and made good time. They reached Woodend just as the rain started. The Gold Escort stopped in the main street whilst John headed to the small local wooden lock up.

The local constable greeted him. "It's good to see you. I'll be glad to get rid of these two. They are trouble. Be careful."

The two prisoners were sullen and looked nasty. John decided to take no chances. He disconnected one handcuff on each Woodend prisoner and locked them onto the rings mounted on the inside wall of the wagon. Each prisoner was effectively chained to the wall and on either side in the wagon.

They wasted no time. With a quick wave to the constable they rode to meet with the Gold Escort in the main street. With their meal break and the tending of the horses, they ran out of time and were soon on the road again.

As soon as they left Woodend they entered the notorious Black Forrest. The Lieutenant warned everyone to be alert although it hardly need be said as they all knew of its reputation.

A mist had descended low on the forest and had reduced forward vision to about two hundred yards. Everyone was nervously peering into the gloom with their hand on their pistols ready for use in case of an ambush.

John was surprised that he was excited by the prospect of danger and the possible drama they could confront as they turned around each bend in the long three mile downhill ride. He was to be disappointed. They did see two horsemen in the distance but they quickly disappeared into the dense forest. As they left the forest the mist lifted almost immediately.

Visibility improved but the rain continued. John could sense the relief from the men that they had not been attacked, particularly in such a dangerous area.

Lieutenant Green advised that he was going to continue nonstop through to Melbourne.

John nodded acceptance; he would be home sooner. The rain had continued on and off since they left Woodend and with low cloud, the day continued grey with limited visibility. They continued at a trot and maintained the same distance from the gold cart. Their horses were fit and could continue this pace for hours. The trip was now starting to become boring and the rain was now very heavy. As they approached the hill above the town of Keilor, John became puzzled as he looked at the wagon.

Under the wagon a shape appeared and dropped to the roadway and then another. He shouted to the constable who was also watching. He could not believe his eyes. Two of the prisoners had escaped from the wagon.

The constable charged his horse at one prisoner. His horse's chest hit him and sent him tumbling. The constable drew his pistol and pointed it at him. He surrendered immediately.

John chased the other prisoner and as he drew level with him, in one action he grabbed him by the collar and lifted him clear of the ground and then let him go.

The prisoner was still trying to keep running but his legs had crossed. He lost his balance, stumbled and crashed head first into a tree. Slightly stunned he staggered to his feet and looked up into John's revolver barrel.

The wagon driver had stopped the horses when he heard the commotion. Lieutenant Green had looked back but the Gold Escort did not stop. He was obeying his orders – 'Not to stop under any circumstance in the countryside'. They were now about half of a mile ahead of the prison wagon.

John chained the two would-be escapees to the rings inside the wagon again. His quick look had not revealed how they had got out through the floor but he would sort that out later. They couldn't get out of the wagon now and he wanted to catch up to the Gold Escort.

A quick canter soon had them back in position behind the Gold Escort.

Lieutenant Green turned and called, "Is everything under control?"

John waved and nodded in reply. He would tell him the story later.

As they travelled through Keilor, a few spectators looked at the small cavalcade but most just continued about their daily business. People, horses, wagons and government officials transited their village daily and were of no particular interest to them. After all, it was the main road to the goldfields.

The rain had abated but it was still cold and miserable riding weather. A few hours ride had them entering the outskirts of Melbourne late in the afternoon. They followed the Gold Escort to the Mint, where the gold was deposited in its vault.

Lieutenant Green and John had a short conversation

at the gates. The lieutenant laughed as John related the escape and capture of the prisoners. He said it would have to be the shortest escape time and the quickest capture ever. They shook hands, wished each other good luck and went their separate ways.

John arrived at the Melbourne Barracks as they were closing the main gate. The two constables unloaded the prisoners and handed them over to the warders.

John reported to the duty inspector, who coincidently had been his previous supervisor – Inspector Alford. They decided to inspect the prison wagon to find out how the prisoners had got out of the wagon. The floor was in four wooden sections and screwed to the wagon's chassis. They could see that all the screws were in place and the wagon walls were intact.

John crawled under the wagon and pushed up on each of the panels. The first three remained in place but he was able to push the last panel upwards. He had discovered the escape method. The panel retaining screws had been sawn off and the screw heads glued into place. How could this have happened to a police wagon? John would investigate the matter further when he returned to Kyneton.

After finalising a few administrative matters, John decided to call it a day. The constables would be staying at the barracks. He had instructed them to tend to the horses, to enjoy their two days off and be ready to leave Monday at eight a.m.

During his trip debrief, Inspector Alford had informed him that three constables would be accompanying his team back to Kyneton, on their way to their postings in Bendigo. They were being sent to help protect the Chinese mining community from the racist attacks being carried out by some of the local goldminers. The attacks were serious and of major concern to the Government.

John headed home knowing that he would surprise his family. It was only a short ride to his home and after leaving his horse at the corner stables he walked down the street to his house. He stood at his front fence looking at the front of the house, admiring Jane's garden.

There were two trees in the centre of the garden surrounded by a mass of flowers of all colours. Rusty, the family dog, saw John standing there and ran at him aggressively but stopped when he heard his name called and looked up at him, wagging his tail.

After opening the gate, John walked to the front door and knocked. George opened the door, surprised and, smiling, stepped to his father and put his arms around him. He called over his shoulder. "Look who's here!"

Jane entered the room and opened her arms. John stepped past George to kiss his wife.

"This is a pleasant surprise. I didn't expect you for a week or so. Have you eaten yet?" He had arrived just as dinner was being served. Jane took him by the arm and led him to the table. Sarah was at a friend's house and staying overnight. He looked forward to seeing her tomorrow.

The three sat up late that night, swapping stories and their thoughts for the future. George was happy in his employment and now had the position of Assistant Duty Manager. His rapid rise was due to a lack of manpower. His colleagues were deserting their employment to go to the goldfields in the hope of quick riches. This had become a major problem, both in Melbourne and the bush. Merchants, the public service, industry and agriculture areas were all suffering from lack of staff.

Jane proudly said, "Sarah has become very skilled

at fitting and sewing dresses under Mrs Jones's tuition. She mentioned to her that I was moving to Kyneton to be with her father and that she might also be going. Mrs Jones has many clients in the Kyneton district and, when she heard this, she asked Sarah if she would be interested in working a few days a week in the town to help her to establish her brand name locally."

Jane continued. "This would not only save her clients the discomfort of travelling by coach all the way to Melbourne and back but could also help increase her local sales. Sarah was pleasantly surprised at the offer and said she would speak with us first but did tell Mrs Jones she was interested."

Saturday dawned cool, sunny with no wind. After breakfast Jane suggested that they go for a walk to town. John readily agreed. He wanted to spend as much quality time as he could with his wife.

George gave them a smile, a wave and went to work. Sarah had not arrived home yet so they had the day to themselves.

Arm in arm they strolled alongside the river. The flowering river gums were plentiful and birds were everywhere. A few aborigines were lounging under trees and small boats were being rowed energetically by fit young seamen taking people to and fro. It was a peaceful scene.

Other couples were out walking and enjoying the good weather. Jane commented that today was the first day in a week that it had not rained.

Jane suddenly stopped and pointed. "That's Sarah over there in the green dress." Jane called and waved to the girl and it was Sarah. She excitedly waved back and hurried across the street. With a happy smile, she kissed her father. "Where did you spring from?"

"I had an assignment in Melbourne and here I am." With Jane on one arm and Sarah on the other, the three happily walked to town to a tea parlour. Sarah sat with her parents and retold them of the offer from her employer. John and Jane were also enthusiastic with the offer. It would be good if they were together. Sarah would eventually marry and the more time they were together now, the longer they could enjoy being a close family unit.

John described the cottage, the stable and the land to them. Jane asked about the possibility of gardens with flowers and vegetables and was pleased with John's positive response. Sarah would need a gig to travel to Kyneton if her new position transpired. Mrs Jones was optimistic; Sarah was also!

The rest of Saturday and all of Sunday were spent talking of their collective future.

Jane started packing. She had some large items that would be loaded into the wagon to save collecting them later.

George would be sorry to see his mother and sister leave. "I'll keep the cottage. I have a friend who can stay here and share the rent with me."

It was decided that Jane would travel to Kyneton with John on Monday morning and Sarah would stay and continue working with Mrs Jones pending the outcome of her Kyneton idea.

Mrs Jones was considering making a lease arrangement whereby she might share a shop for a few days a week to see if her plan was viable.

John immediately thought of talking with William Miles. In his capacity as Mayor he would know of any shopkeeper worth talking with. He would discuss it with William before he said anything to Sarah.

The family enjoyed the weekend. George and Sarah

had some friends visit Sunday afternoon, for tea.

John was impressed by the confidence the younger people had in their future in this emerging Colony. Each had employment, was smartly dressed and well mannered. Naturally the Victorian temperate climate had influenced their attire. Light colours and materials were today's fashion together with sun protection headwear.

CHAPTER EIGHT

Woodlea

A chilly Monday morning dawned with a distant rooster waking the family at sunrise. There were no clouds and only a slight breeze. It promised to be a typical late winter's day.

After a quick breakfast, John left to meet his constables and the wagon. Jane was to travel on the wagon seated alongside a constable while John and the remaining entourage would form up with two constables leading and the other two bringing up the rear.

John would ride alongside the wagon. There was no particular reason for this formation except that its precise military appearance looked professional to passers-by.

Jane and the children were waiting at the cottage gate. After loading Jane's luggage, John went inside the cottage and came back with his leather boxing bag and gave it to George. "This was my lucky charm. It's now yours. I hope it brings you the good fortune that I have had."

After a few quick hugs and kisses, John and his

team headed out of Melbourne. Their first stop was Keilor for a quick break and a meal. He wanted to make Kyneton by nightfall. The further north they travelled up into the Macedon Ranges the colder it became. Jane was prepared and had wrapped herself in a lamb skin cloak and bonnet. The troopers had their capes.

The trip through the Black Forest was uneventful. Several other travellers formed up behind them. No doubt they felt more secure in the presence of six armed policemen.

They had another quick stop in Woodend and then onto Kyneton. They were making good time, so John asked Jane if she wanted to go to the cottage tonight; if not, they could stay at an hotel.

"No, let's go to the cottage."

John nodded. He had guessed she would.

They arrived at the barracks late afternoon. John helped Jane from the wagon and took her into the office and left her at his desk as he dismissed his own constables and settled the Bendigo constables in their overnight quarters.

William had previously offered John the use of the gig he had found in the stables. After a good clean, John had checked the harness and greased wheel hubs. It was ready for use again. He also installed a shotgun slot under the seat and purchased a pony for the gig, suitable for Jane to handle. John had brought the gig into the barracks several weeks beforehand for an occasion such as this – to drive Jane to the cottage.

After harnessing his horse into the gig and loading her luggage, they headed to their new home. It was no longer just a cottage. It was Woodlea, their home.

John halted the horse at the top of the hill where William had first shown him the property. The full moon showed the cottage, its trees and the surrounding hills to advantage. The soft shadows complemented a picturesque, serene scene.

They sat quietly. John waited for Jane to speak.

She looked at John and then kissed him. "I could never have imagined such a sight. It's beautiful. Let's go to our new home."

John stopped at the cottage door, opened it and then carried her across the threshold. He had candles in every room and once these were lit, the cottage came alive.

Jane walked slowly through each room. "With curtains, wall hangings and flowers this will definitely be our home." That night they relived their early times together. The stillness of the Australian bush was a new world for her.

Jane quickly settled into the ways of a country wife. She soon learnt how to harness their pony to the gig and after a few lessons from John she began to drive the gig into Kyneton to do the weekly shopping.

John introduced her to one or two ladies he had met. She quickly made friends and soon felt that she had become a member of the community. No doubt John's status in the town helped her acceptance.

Jane began to plan the gardens – flowers to surround the cottage and she halved the remaining section, one for fruit trees and one for vegetables. At weekends John would break the topsoil and during the week Jane would sow and water the seeds. It was slow progress but they were both optimistic that their efforts would be successful.

John had brought two young dogs of unknown breeding but they were big and noisy. He named them Jack and Jill. He had two long wires laid around the cottage. One wire was alongside two walls and the other alongside the opposite two walls. The ends of the wires were attached to the corners of the opposite walls. The dogs could run around each of their two walls with their chain sliding along the wire. Either dog could stop an intruder approaching close to the cottage. Jane became their favourite and they followed her everywhere when they were unchained.

The investigation into the loose panel on the wagon revealed one of the cartwright's workers had been a brother of one of the prisoners. He had not returned to work after the police wagon wheel had been repaired and had since left the district.

The Kyneton Police Force was having a quiet month; even the locals were law abiding.

"This won't last; we'll have a drama soon," commented Inspector Brittan.

Next day they received a letter from the Kilmore Barracks advising that there were four bushrangers in their area. They had bailed up four groups of travellers over the last week. Although shots had been fired, no one had been injured but they needed to be caught. Kilmore requested a police presence in the area between Kilmore and Kyneton.

The area was heavily treed and with numerous hills. It was difficult terrain to traverse but it had to be done. The Inspector briefed John and told him to select two troopers and prepare to be ready to leave the next morning for a week's search.

Jane wasn't too happy about being alone for a week. But she had the two dogs, security shutters and a shotgun behind the front door. John had taught her to fire the gun but she didn't enjoy the vicious recoil.

"You won't have to shoot anyone. The noise will frighten them away," said John.

Once she fired at a fox near the fowl house. The noise caused the dogs to begin barking, the chooks to go berserk, the sheep to run down to the river and she hurt her shoulder.

John impressed on her she would be safe, although he was little nervous himself leaving her.

Inspector Brittan offered to visit her every few days.

John left Jane standing quietly on the doorstep with the dogs sitting unchained at her feet.

John and his two constables, Bradley and Moore, left the barracks midmorning. Each constable carried a six shot revolver and a double barrel shotgun. John had a revolver and a carbine. The team took a single horse light cart driven by Constable Bradley with a spare horse tied to the tailgate.

The cart was loaded with camping gear, cooking equipment, an adequate supply of food, water and horse fodder. They headed east on a balmy summer day on roads that were dry and dusty. After two hours, with dry throats, they stopped for a breather.

Two horsemen waved to them and approached. John and his men were cautious and waited until they were close before he shouted to them to identify themselves.

"I'm Stan Pattinson of Hilton farm."

Constable Moore waved to him. "Yes, I know him."

John nodded. "What can we do for you?"

Stan Pattinson was a farmer in their search area. "You might like to check out four horsemen upstream of that creek." He pointed north towards a gully. "They are not locals and they've been camping there for a few days and are avoiding locals. They seem suspicious to me."

John nodded. "We'll ride up the gully and have a look. Thank you." They nodded to each and went their separate ways.

They hid the cart behind some bushes after tying the horse to a tree.

The ride up the gully was mainly in clear shallow water lined by reeds. Birds flittered in the trees and sunlight glistened on the green leaves.

Constable Bradley stopped suddenly and pointed to a wisp of smoke rising slowly into the air.

John signalled them to dismount quietly. With their revolvers drawn the three crept along the creek bed. Suddenly a carbine shot rang out in the still bush.

Constable Bradley collapsed into the water. Shouts echoed in the bushes and trees followed by crashes made by horses and riders fleeing. John briefly saw a rider wearing a cabbage tree hat fleeing on a light brown horse with white patches and then the horseman vanished into the forest.

Constable Moore went to help Bradley. He was bleeding badly from a bullet wound in his thigh. The priority was now the injured constable, the horsemen mattered not.

Constable Moore told John to press his hand down hard on the centre of the bleeding, while he scooped up two handfuls of dried mud from the side of the creek. He pressed this mud onto the wound and told John to cut the injured Bradley's shirt into several six inch wide strips.

When John handed him the strips, he tied them tightly over the mud pack. The bleeding had stopped but Bradley could not be placed on a horse. They needed the cart. John rode back and brought the cart up the creek bed without too much trouble.

They made Bradley as comfortable as possible in the cart and headed to Kilmore, which was the closest town. It was an uncomfortable ride for him even though he was lying on a folded up tent, their bedding and straw.

When they arrived in Kilmore, the doctor was in his surgery. After a quick inspection he commented, "Whoever did this dressing saved the man's life. The mud and the tight strips was a perfect method to stop the bleeding. The bulled nicked a major artery. Well done, Sergeant."

"It wasn't me; it was Constable Moore here," said John.

They both looked at Moore enquiringly. He answered, "I served with the British Army in India and saw many similar bullet wounds so I knew immediately the urgency to stop major bleeding. There was plenty of clean creek mud handy and, besides, he's my mate; I had to do a good job."

Bradley's recuperation period could only be guessed – a month or two?

John and Constable Moore headed back to Kyneton the next day with Moore driving the cart with the two horses trotting behind. Inwardly John was angry with himself for allowing Bradley to be shot, although he knew there was always a risk during this type of duty.

They made good time to the small town of Lancefield and stopped at the local stables to feed and water the horses. The town had a wide street with an inn, a few stores and a small dilapidated school.

Constable Moore grabbed John by his arm and nodded to the end stall. There was a skewbald horse, light brown with white patches. John casually commented on the horse's markings to the stable hand.

"The owner's in the inn over there," he replied.

Constable Moore snatched up his shotgun, put it under his arm and walked towards the inn.

John called him to wait. The inn door was open and they could see several patrons leaning on the bar. At the far end of the bar were four men, one wearing a cabbage tree hat. Two were young and the last was a large bearded man. John walked towards the group of four, his hand on his revolver. Moore was alongside him with the shotgun in his hands.

The cabbage tree hat man saw them approaching and pulled out his pistol but Moore fired his shotgun first. The charge hit him in the chest. The impact lifted him off his feet and sent him flying backwards into a wall. He slid to the floor – dead.

The two young men turned and ran out, heading into the trees south of the inn. The fourth man angrily ran at John, who stepped sideways and hit the assailant behind the ear with the butt of his revolver. He dropped forward, unconscious, hitting his face on the dirt floor, breaking his nose and splitting an eye brow.

The excitement was over quickly; some patrons were still drinking their ales. Not a drop was spilt. The bush Colonials were a tough breed.

Others picked up their ales and walked over to inspect the dead man, shrugged their shoulders then went back to their place at the bar. They all agreed he was not a local.

When the fourth man regained consciousness he realised he was handcuffed and lying in the cart ready to go to the Kyneton gaol. When interviewed he said he was the dead man's brother and they were itinerant shearers down on their luck.

The two young men were deserters from a ship in Hobson's Bay and weren't real bushrangers. They were looking for some cash to travel to Sydney.

The brothers had given them defective pistols, unable to fire. They hadn't trusted them.

When John heard this, he lost all interest in pursuing them. The forests were too dense for tracking. He doubted their chances of survival.

An enterprising drinker asked, "What's going to happen to their horses?" It was a good question. Only the skewbald was branded and the stable hand offered to stable it until the owner could be found. The other three horses were unbranded. The prisoner said they stole the three of them from a paddock with a large mob of brumbies, just broken in, somewhere north of the Murray River. He had no idea who owned them.

Several weeks later John received a letter from Ivan Scott, the skewbald horse owner. He lived near Stan Pattinson on Emerald Farm. Stan had seen the horse in the barn during a shopping visit for supplies and had told him the story. The horse had been a present for Ivan's son's twentieth birthday. The letter was a 'Thank you'.

The three horses were underfed and needed shoeing. John was not interested in taking them to Kyneton in their current condition. He looked at the school and said to the innkeeper, "Auction them and give the money to the school teacher. I can see he needs money to do some repairs. Agreed?"

The innkeeper nodded and shook John's hand. "Leave the burial to us; we'll handle it."

John nodded. "Good, that's one job I don't want."

Constable Moore didn't like bouncing around on the cart seat and suggested that the prisoner do the driving. John nodded and they headed west again, getting closer to home. The remainder of the trip was uneventful.

The prisoner sat quietly in the cart, holding the reins. The horse just followed the road while John and the constable rode behind, with their own thoughts.

The Inspector was shocked to learn that one of his constables had been shot. On the other hand he was delighted his men had broken up the gang. The prisoner was sent to Melbourne on the next Bendigo Police 'Black Maria'.

The two escapees were of no interest to the Inspector. "Mention them in your report but forget them. We're not wasting time searching for them," he instructed.

CHAPTER NINE

Challenges

Jane kept herself busy. For relaxation she would use her skills on petit point and crocheting, making dollies and pillow slips. Her gardening efforts were a surprise. The light rains and the sunshine capped off her seed sowing efforts and already plants were growing. Even the vegetable beds had small green growths erupting through the soil. She had found the watering laborious, but now she thought it was worth the effort.

Over the weekends John had chopped plenty of firewood for the stove. Jane was a capable cook. Today she was baking bread and scones.

The stove was used for cooking, boiling washing water, heating, drying clothes and even to heat the clothes iron.

While waiting for the bread to bake and during ironing their clothes, she noticed two horsemen on the top road looking towards the farm. They only stayed there for a few minutes but it concerned her. She made a mental note to be watchful. Even with the gun and the dogs she was still nervous without John home.

The next day the dogs started barking. Jane looked out of the kitchen window and saw the same two men riding up to the front gate. They did not dismount but nodded to Jane. "Is your husband home, Missus? We're looking for work."

Jane answered, "We do our own work."

"Can you give us a cuppa? It's been dry on the road," one rider asked.

She replied firmly, "No, please go, or I'll set the dogs on you."

They sat there for a few minutes looking around and could see the dogs were chained on two long lines. Jane reached behind the door and brought out the shotgun and levelled it them.

Without a word they turned and trotted back down to the road. Jane went inside, slightly shaken, and had a cup of tea. She felt proud of the way she managed the unwelcome visitors and felt John would be too.

Late that night, the dogs began to bark loudly and woke Jane. They were straining their chains. The shutters were all in place. She was secure.

She looked through the peephole.

With the help of the moonlight she could see the shadow of two figures moving towards the stable and two horses tied near its open door. One man stood by the stable door holding a gun and unsaddling one of their horses, while the other started to pull the gig out.

Jane realised that they intended to steal her gig. With the shotgun under her arm she opened the front door and went to Jack and unclipped his chain and then to Jill and unclipped her chain.

The dogs ran off, jumped the picket fence and raced to the stable. The robbers had not expected Jane to leave the safety of the cottage, let alone come outside to release her dogs. Both of them ran inside the stable pulling the door closed when they realised the dogs were loose.

In his panic, the man with the gun, dropped it. Jane ran behind the dogs and dropped the stable outside latch bar into its lock. The robbers were not only trapped in the stable. They had no way of bypassing the unchained dogs outside.

Jane left the dogs loose and went back to the cottage and locked the front door. She sat there shaking. A cup of tea helped settle her nerves. She finally dozed off in her favourite lounge chair.

When she awoke with a start, it was daytime. She quickly dressed and went outside with the shotgun. The mail coach normally went past on the top road not long after dawn and she wanted to attract the driver's attention.

As expected the coach appeared on time. Jane fired the shotgun and the coach slowed down and came down her drive. The driver thought it was a great joke and couldn't stop laughing. He said he would go straight to Inspector Brittan and tell him she needed his help. With a crack of his whip the coach headed for Kyneton.

Jane could hear the robbers pleading for her to release them. Their pleas fell on deaf ears. One of their horses was still tied to the rail. She fed and watered him. The unsaddled one had wandered down to the river through the slip rails which were down and was happily grazing. He had plenty of grass and water.

An hour or so after the coach had departed, up galloped the Inspector and two armed constables. His first words were, "Are you alright? Are you unharmed?"

Jane smiled. "Yes, but stay mounted while I tie up the dogs. I don't want any policemen bitten." When the dogs were back on their running lines, they all went to the stable. Jane lifted the latch bar and stepped back as the police took over and opened the door.

The Constable and the Miner

Two miserable would-be robbers sat forlornly on hay bales. The constables laughingly handcuffed them. They sat them on their remaining horse and took them to Kyneton gaol.

The Inspector stayed for a while, listening to Jane's story and, after satisfying himself that she felt comfortable staying at the cottage by herself, he left for town.

The next morning she walked down to the horse in the trees by the river. It still had its bridle fitted. Jane was able to lead him back and put him in a stall. He was limping a little. One of his shoes was only held on by one nail. She discovered he was unbranded. She would wait for John. He would know what to do with the horse.

The story soon got around the district. It was – Don't mess with the Police Sergeant's wife and her dogs at Woodlea Farm! She's a tough woman.

John knew nothing of his wife's exploits until he walked into the barracks. He had received several hearty waves when riding up the main street and had just waved back, not realising his wife's new found notoriety.

When Inspector Brittan told John the story, he was at first shocked and then relieved.

After the quick debrief he had left the barracks and galloped for home. He first saw her in the vegetable garden, a watering can in her hand with not a care in the world. The dogs were loose and wrestling each other on the grass. He shook his head. What a woman!

They kissed and hugged each other. John felt guilty.

Jane said, "I was safe. Think about it. The dogs, the shutters and the shotgun. I knew I could handle them."

John relaxed and dropped the subject. He didn't

want to dent her confidence. She was right, but John wished it had not happened. They had two days together, mainly in the gardens.

The robbers' horses posed a problem. They had too many horses at the barracks now. It served as the local pound for unbranded and branded strays. The Inspector didn't want to know about it and told John to keep the horse at Woodlea.

Doing his patrols around town now took a lot longer. Every second person enquired after his wife's health. A quick chat, a smile and a hand shake with each meeting. This continued for nearly two weeks.

A letter from Sarah reminded him to see William Miles regarding a retail outlet for Mrs Jones. He visited William at the Mayoral Office and found him heading out for lunch with another man. He invited John to join them and introduced him as Geoffrey Marsh, "A leading local business man."

Reluctantly John agreed; he felt he was intruding. Unbeknown to him the two of them had just completed plans to expand the local emporium. During lunch, listening to them discussing these plans, John took the opportunity to ask, "Could a small dressmaker be accommodated in your expansion? My daughter's employer is interested in having another shop here."

William answered, "Yes, we need small businesses to provide a variety under one roof."

Geoffrey nodded. "Ask her to contact me so we can discuss what she needs and what we can offer." The chance lunch was enjoyed by all.

That night he wrote to Sarah giving her Geoffrey's contact details for Mrs Jones' follow up action.

Within a fortnight both Mrs Jones and Sarah arrived in Kyneton to meet with Mr Marsh. They soon decided a ladies' wear area would be appropriate in one corner, hat sales in the middle and men's wear in the other corner. The three clothing sections would occupy one wall and complement each other.

The following week the two women returned from Melbourne with stock and display stands and commenced to layout their display. Meanwhile Jane had been preparing the second bedroom for Sarah. She would enjoy her company, particularly when John was away.

The horse from the robbery had been put out to graze in the paddock behind the stable. She was a six year old mare, surprisingly docile and would come to Jane for a pat. She named her Clare. Why, she did not know; it was on a whim.

John had harnessed her in the gig. She was a bit agitated for a week or two. When she had settled down, she trotted very smartly, with her head up and with a high knee lift gait. Before they could drive her any distance she needed shoeing. It was planned that Sarah would rotate the mare and pony in the gig, to travel into the emporium and also to exercise the horses. John installed a third rear facing seat in the gig on the remote chance they all needed to travel together.

John had met Sean, the new blacksmith-farrier when he was shoeing some of the police horses. During a chat he mentioned that he had three horses of his own, an adopted horse and his wife, Jane, had a pony. Two needed shoeing.

Sean interrupted, "Look, I have a mare that needs some exercising. If you wish, I'll ride out to you one weekend."

John nodded. "Yes, I'll be home next weekend. Does that suit you?"

"I'll see you Saturday. I know where you live," replied Sean.

John noted that he was young, presentable, tall and strongly built. He knew Sean had been mining in the Heathcote district, and had arrived in Kyneton three months ago when he was employed by the local blacksmith.

Sean's skills had soon become apparent and he attracted more work to the business. He worked as a harness and saddle repairer, a blacksmith and a farrier.

The current blacksmith was over seventy years of age and only wanted to work part time. He had offered Sean a partnership. They would share the profits now and after twelve months, he would give him half the business. They shook hands on the agreement. The owner had been impressed with his skills, deliberate speech and smiling demeanour.

Sean was pleased with the invitation to visit a farm. All his work so far had been in town. Except for a few country rides, Jess had been sitting in a stable and definitely needed some lengthy exercise. Saturday dawned with the sun shining, a gentle breeze and the magpies warbling. It promised to be a great day. He had now developed a quiet confidence due to his fortunate financial position and a solid business potential. He was a young man with his life in front of him. He was humming a tune to himself as he approached Woodlea.

Smoke was slowly rising from the cottage and he could see a woman in the garden and two dogs running around behind a picket fence. As Sean rode down the track the two dogs began barking. The woman looked up, saw him and chained the dogs. She gave him a friendly wave and called out to the cottage. "John, we have a visitor."

As Sean dismounted, John appeared from behind the stable. "Welcome. I see you've brought good weather with you. This is my wife, Jane. Jane, this is Sean."

They shook hands.

Jane said, "We were expecting you. I have cooked some scones. Please join us in tea before you begin working."

Sean could see the female touch inside the cottage – curtains on the windows, pictures and flower in vases. He felt a touch of nostalgia, remembering his home as a boy. He could see that Jane and John were devoted to each other and content with life. Jane was the conversationalist, asking Sean where he was from and what he thought of Australia. Sean spoke briefly of his mining days, his voyage and his gamble at mining. He did not comment on his good fortune. He just said, "I'm happy and enjoying my life in Kyneton."

John interrupted. "I think it's time to check the horses. I'll call our daughter, Sarah, to bring up the pony. She has him down by the river."

Jane walked Sean to the stable. Two horses were in separate stalls and he could see they were well fed. Nice glossy coats and strong withers.

As he was wearing visiting clothes, he had brought his leather apron to protect them when shoeing the horses. Clare was the first to be shod. All her shoes were removed and new ones fitted, with the metal nails cut back and filed. The outside of the hooves, too, were filed. He was quick. As he finished, Sarah walked the pony into the barn.

"This is Sean and this is Sarah," introduced John. They nodded to each then and shook hands, each looking as if assessing the other.

Sarah handed the reins to Sean and stood alongside him. Sean quickly got to work, off with the worn shoes and on with new ones. John's horse's shoes were in good order.

As they left the stable, Sarah walked alongside Sean. "I work three shops down from you in the

Emporium. I often see you busy working, your head down, hammering away."

"Next time call me so I can say hello. I'm won't be that busy," said Sean.

Sarah replied laughingly, "I'll call loudly." After chatting for a short time, Sean made the comment that he was looking to put Jess out to pasture. He felt it was wrong keeping her in a stable.

He then took his leave. He shook hands, mounted Jess and rode down the track. As he neared the road he turned, waved and headed back to town.

Sarah turned to her parents. "I like him. I'm going to marry him one day."

Jane and John stood there absorbing her words in silence. They knew she was strong willed. This comment was surprising, but not disturbing.

Sean rode back, thinking of Sarah. She was a pretty young woman and he was impressed by her confidence. Although he had met very few women, he felt that she was special and wondered how he could meet with her again.

That evening, during dinner, Jane asked, "How much did Sean charge for shoeing the horses?"

"Oh! I forgot to ask him. I'll see him on Monday."

Sarah piped up. "Why not offer him to leave his horse here instead. Then I can see more of him."

John laughed. "Yes, I'll mention it on Monday."

When John discussed the suggestion concerning Jess, Sean readily agreed. He realised it would give him an excuse to see more of Sarah. There were horses at the blacksmith stables he could borrow to take Jess out.

Many small Victorian towns had formed agricultural associations for the local farmers and graziers to show

The Constable and the Miner

their animals and products and compete in various class awards. These awards ranged from livestock, birds, vegetables, cakes and needlework, to name a few. Other more energetic competitions were shearing, buck jumping and equestrian events.

These Agriculture Association Show Days required a police presence. Mostly the crowd was well behaved but often a few of the patrons would become boisterous and annoying due to excessive alcohol consumption. As usual, a large beer tent with wall panels had been assembled at the Show Ground. It was a hot day and the bar was well patronised.

John was standing watching the shearing competition when a farmer ran up and grabbed him by the arm. "I think you're needed at the beer tent."

The two of them walked quickly to the tent. As they drew closer, they could hear someone shouting. "Put that bloody snake back in the bag!"

John stood at the back of a laughing crowd and looked over their heads.

He saw an angry barman yelling at a drunken shearer who was leaning on a wall partition with a bag in one hand and holding a snake on the bar in his other. The snake's head was raised and looking around. The shearer was ranting. "All I want is a jug of beer and I'll put back him in the bag."

The barman was furious. "Do it now or else!"

The shearer started to rant again.

The barman reached under the counter, pulled out a shotgun and fired at the head of the snake. The snake's head was splattered over the wooden partition.

The drunken shearer stared at remainder of the snake. "He was my mate."

The barman came around the bar, grabbed him by the neck and waist belt and bodily threw him out onto the grass and walked back and went back serving as if nothing had happened.

John shook his head and walked back to watch the shearing competition. He didn't consider the incident warranted any police involvement.

The following week, Inspector Brittan called John into his office. He invited him to sit down. "Williams, Melbourne have asked me to loan you, for a period of one month. They believe your experience in London will help to resolve a problem they are having. I have agreed with their request. You are due for a promotion and this task could be to your advantage. They said you will be provided with married quarters and an off duty Cobb and Co. coach travel pass to travel home, or you can ride your horse if you wish.

"You will leave in three days. Good luck in the challenge they have for you. Before you ask, I don't know anymore."

Jane was not very impressed at first but then said she would come to Melbourne for a few days. It would give her a chance to see more of George. Sarah was non-committal; she had Sean.

CHAPTER TEN

The Pick Pockets

John decided to ride his horse to Melbourne. After it was stabled he reported to the duty inspector, who directed him to Special Projects Inspector Alford, his previous mentor. They greeted each other as old friends. After a few pleasant words and enquiring sentences, they got down to business.

Melbourne city was experiencing a plague of pick pocketing. The city was growing at an alarming rate and the increase in the reports of these robberies was causing extreme embarrassment to the police and the Commissioner wanted it stopped.

The gold rush boom period was over but Melbourne's population was still increasing at an alarming rate, as was its crime rate. Inspector Alford had recommended John as the man to head up the task force.

John sat silent. Yes, he had experience with the problem in London but he had only been a constable in those days. He thought for a while before he answered. "I would like a few hours to give this some thought. Can I meet with you this afternoon?"

The Inspector nodded, and pointed. "Yes. One o'clock. Here. You can use that office over there."

John placed a page in front of him and started to think, and then began to write. This flood of pickpocketing was probably well organised. He assumed the organiser would be based in the city and pickpockets would have limited transport, if any. Jewellery, watches, snuff boxes, money and gold chains etc. would need a fence, most probably the organiser, to sell them illegally.

He believed he would need undercover policemen positioned in key locations. John decided to set up an incident board covering the mile square of the city and mark where every known robbery had occurred and at what time. This should give him areas where and when to concentrate his men. When a pickpocket was spotted he would not be arrested as was being done now. The undercover police officer would follow the culprit.

John wanted to focus on locating the organiser. Deciding the number of men needed would be determined by the crime concentrations identified on the incident board.

When John reported back to Inspector Alford's office, there were three other inspectors present.

After introductions, he presented his plan. "I want two men now to start the incident board. By tomorrow morning I will know what manpower I need."

Surprisingly, they all agreed and acknowledged that arresting them had made no difference to the robbery rate. The fines were not a deterrent. To locate and break up the organisation they had needed a realistic plan. They now had one.

Next morning two policemen were in his office when he arrived. Inspector Alford had selected two constables, James Stirling and Peter Evans who were both educated and enthusiastic. Within four hours they had every known robbery over the past twelve months marked on the planning board. It revealed four hotspots covering ninety percent of the incidents and all had occurred in the morning between ten o'clock and noon and in the afternoon between three o'clock and four o'clock. James and Peter were surprised. They thought the robberies were random and spread all over the city throughout the day.

John now had facts to decide his manpower requirements. The three of them sat down and discussed each other's ideas. It was decided they would have three teams of three men. They would roster the three teams through the four areas daily at the identified times and report back after four o'clock or if they had identified a culprit and were following him or her, report to John, before leaving for home.

Selecting the men for his team was done quietly and with care. They were seeking men who would blend in with the crowd, not slim, heavy, sallow complexion or with large beards. Men who had served in the Melbourne police force for over two years also were not considered.

It took two days but the project was operational within a week and Inspector Alford was happy to report this to the Commissioner who informed the Premier. The project was kept secret from the rank and file in the police force. They were concerned about possible police corruption.

The task force had limited success the first few days, losing three suspects near the main market place. It was a very busy area with over fifty meat and vegetable stalls. They were confident that they would home in the organisation, though.

James mentioned that here were three inns in the area. Two were disreputable and known haunts of criminals. John and James Stirling visited the inns and purchased ales, posing as itinerant workers.

The first inn was small and only consisted of three rooms. The second inn – The Viking – was much larger with several rooms for overnight stayers.

John went to the bar and collected two ales and as he was being handed his change by the barman, he saw a sight he had not seen since The Old Bailey – a right hand with the first two fingers missing. Darcy Sykes was free and living in Melbourne and running an inn. When John looked at him he could recognise his features. He appeared much older, but it was him. When they sat down James asked if something was wrong.

John told him the story and James asked, "Would he be capable of organising a pickpocket racket?"

"Well, he was a thug and robber but he was a loner. I doubt it."

James turned quickly and lowered his head. "See the drinker at the far end of the bar with the brown forage cap talking to Sykes, he's a local councillor. Let's get out of here. He knows me."

John had a quick look at them as Darcy and the councillor left the bar and entered a side room.

They walked back to the barracks in silence. John was wondering if they had accidently discovered the organisation ring leaders. They had no evidence to warrant raiding The Viking. They would still have to follow a suspect pickpocket into the inn to catch them with stolen goods. He was satisfied the first week had been productive.

Jane came down for the weekend and they arranged to dine at a restaurant with George. They were both surprised to see him enter the dining room accompanied by an attractive young lady. John stood and shook George's hand and turned to the lady who George introduced as Bridget Keough.

Jane kissed George and greeted Bridget. The women

sat together and Jane soon had Bridget comfortable and chatting.

Bridget was from County Clare and had emigrated with her family five years earlier. Her father was a stonemason, building the bluestone houses being erected throughout the immediate Melbourne area. She had a delightful Irish brogue and her reddish hair showed she was from the west coast.

George was looking healthy and happy. He was enjoying his work and had settled into the local life style. He had joined the local cricket and rowing clubs as an active member.

John sat back and enjoyed listening to the conversation and only occasionally spoke.

The week had been demanding and he was tired, mentally and physically. The meal was first class as was the cost, but it was worth it. They left together, John and Jane heading to the barracks and George escorting Bridget home to Collingwood.

John and Jane walked arm in arm. They were enjoying each other's company. Both of their children had grown up and were possibly heading for marriage. Life was pleasantly moving along for them all.

The second week, John and his task force were working the areas during the times identified, while other constables were catching a few culprits, as per normal, and not disrupting John's undercover operation.

Two days after their visit to The Viking, Peter Evans ran up to John in street. "Quick, follow me. We have seen a pickpocket rob a purse from a gentleman and he's sitting at the corner next to the inn eating a sandwich. I think we should follow him. If he enters The Viking we will have cause to raid it."

"Yes, I'll go ahead and sit in the bar and wait for you. Bring your team and mine. It may become physical," said John.

John ordered an ale and sat looking out of the window. Sykes had served him but John no longer had his beard and he wasn't recognised. He spotted Peter approaching, walking two paces behind a short stocky lad. The other task force members were close behind.

Sykes saw the lad at the inn doorway and motioned him to come into the bar. He and the lad then went into a side room and closed the door.

John waited for two minutes and then signalled his men to enter the inn and crash open the bar side room door.

Sykes stood there, dumbfounded. He knew they were policemen. Then he turned to the lad. "You fool, you were followed." He picked up a bronze stature and struck him on the head. The lad fell unconscious to the ground. Evans and his men immediately wrestled Sykes to the floor.

John told the patrons to have a drink 'on the house' and then leave. They cheered and there was no violence. The injured lad sat up and started to cry. John told him to go home and not rob again or else. The lad soon scampered away, his head bleeding from his wound.

When the team searched the room they found several metal lockers filled with stolen goods. The purse seen by Peter Evans was on a table. The raid had been successful.

John sent one of his team to bring Inspector Alford to the inn.

He wanted to interview Sykes away from prying eyes and not have the councillor alerted. When the Inspector arrived John briefed him on the events of the previous days including seeing the councillor with Sykes.

When the interview started, Sykes still had not recognised John. Sykes could not deny the charge of 'Possessing stolen Goods' but denied selling them and said he would be killed if he revealed the organiser; he had powerful connections.

"Darcy, we already know he's the local councillor," said John.

Sykes nodded. "Yes, you're right." Then he looked intently at John. "I'm sure I know you."

"You said we would meet again when we last met in London. I'm The Toff, Constable John Williams from the Old Dart.

"Now would you mind telling us how this pickpocket racket was organised? Your answer may help to reduce your sentence."

Sykes stared at John, remembering those days at The Old Bailey. He then related the whole robbery set up.

The councillor was the ring leader and was selling the goods to ships' captains and their crews. They had chosen the areas and specific times near banks when they were busiest. They sent in young lads to do the robberies as they were quick and soon vanished into the crowds. John wondered why these ideas had not been considered before.

Inspector Alford arranged for an inspector to arrest the councillor at his home and to search it for stolen goods.

The councillor admitted his role; he had no choice after a considerable quantity of identifiable stolen goods was found in his possession. Sykes was taken to the barrack cells to await trial. The head of the snake was gone. There was nowhere else for the lads to sell their stolen goods. The pickpocketing plague was over, although it would never be stopped completely.

The next day the team sat together to complete a report. The men spent all day recalling the details of the task force's actions, culminating in the arrest and the interview.

The Commissioner was delighted, as was the Premier. The Commissioner said to Inspector Alford. "I want Williams promoted to Sub Inspector and to assume that position in Kyneton. Retire the incumbent Sub Inspector. He's been on sick leave long enough. Also put a note of 'Well done' on Stirling and Evans' files."

John was all smiles when he left Inspector Alford's office.

Now that the assignment had been completed, he was heading home.

He had said good bye to Stirling and Evans and was talking with Inspector Alford when the duty inspector walked in.

"Excuse me. I have just had a message from the Keilor Sergeant concerning a bail up at the Inverness Inn on the Sunbury Road. He has the bushranger locked up but the witness has vanished. Would you mind going via the inn on your way home and talk with the innkeeper. He has the robber locked up in his storeroom. He has admitted to the hold up, but it's a bit confusing. You may be able to find out what really happened."

John nodded. "Certainly, it will be my pleasure to help. I'll send you a report no matter what I find."

The inspector turned and left John to farewell his friend.

"Good bye until next time." They both laughed and waved as he rode out of the barracks.

At noon he stopped at Essendon for a meal and then headed north, past the Keilor turn off, direct to Tullamarine and an hour later was at the Inverness Inn.

The innkeeper was a jolly chap. He reminded John of a typical English publican. When John introduced himself and told him why he was there, he ushered him to a table, after pouring two ales.

He said he first knew of the bail up when two farmers rode up with a man tied to the saddle on a magnificent chestnut mare. The innkeeper agreed to have the bushranger locked up in his storeroom until a constable arrived from Keilor. The farmers were starting to tell the innkeeper what they knew, when a pony in a gig trotted up with a dainty lady holding the reins with a large dog seated alongside her. The farmers told him to ask her what had happened.

The innkeeper offered her a cup of tea while she told him her story. "The bushranger appeared from behind a tree, on a bend, about a mile from the inn. He waved a pistol at me and demanded my purse. I refused and called him a ruffian and told him to get out of my way. The bushranger fired a shot into the air, intending to frighten me. Instead I got angry and released my dog. He ran at the horse and bit it on the leg. The horse reared, throwing the bushranger onto his head."

She continued. "He lay on the road unconscious with my dog standing guard over him. The pistol shot had alerted the two farmers who were riding about half a mile from the bend. When they arrived they lifted the still unconscious bushranger onto his horse and brought him to your inn and I see that you have locked him in your storeroom."

John asked, "What happened to her?" The innkeeper shrugged his shoulders. "I went back to the farmers, had a few ales with them in the bar. She was in another room. When we went looking for her, she had vanished and so had the chestnut mare. It was a nice three year old mare and, believe it or not, it was unbranded, one of the farmers told me. Good luck to her I say. One thing I remember was the gig was red and it had writing on both sides. It had the word 'Hollybrook' in gold print."

John had heard enough to be able to write a report detailing the crime for the prosecutor to use.

A month later, John was at a picnic race meeting. He and Constable Moore were showing a police presence. They didn't expect any trouble. They would probably talk to a few drunks as usual but mainly they would just watch the races. As they walked through the carriage park he noticed a red gig with the words 'Hollybrook' on its sides.

He decided he would like to meet with the owner and ask her about the horse. Constable Moore and he decided to take turns watching out for the owner.

The second last race was won by a chestnut mare. John was watching as the trophy was presented to a small, well dressed woman. He followed her to the stables and saw her walk to the chestnut and then patted her.

"Hello, you have an excellent horse. Where did you buy her?" he asked.

She looked at John with a twinkle in her eye. "She was a present. Wasn't I lucky?" smiled and walked away.

John went to the red gig and waited for her. She was leading the mare and nodded to him. He walked to the mare and looked closely at the brand. It was still healing. John told her who he was and wished her good luck. As far as he was concerned the horse was hers.

"Was this the reason you left the inn without telling anyone?"

"The bushranger was caught. I had had my cup of tea and told my story. There was no reason for me to stay any longer, and yes, I took the horse as compensation."

John smiled, tipped his hat to her, mounted his horse and joined Constable Moore to ride home. The mystery of who had owned the horse previously was never solved.

CHAPTER ELEVEN

Achievers All

The relationship between Sean and Sarah strengthened. They met during the weekends and went riding together around the district. The countryside was conducive to making people happy. The green fields, golden crops, livestock and meandering creeks contributed to a picture of serenity with the happy couple in the middle of the scene.

It was inevitable that they would become engaged to be married.

Sean asked John for her hand in marriage. Naturally John said, "Yes."

Jane and John were nearly as happy as Sean and Sarah with her selection of a husband and looked forward to the coming nuptials.

The formal announcement of their engagement was to be made at the Mechanics Institute Hall. Jane and Sarah wanted it to be a momentous occasion and, after they prepared the invitation list, it seemed most of the district would be attending.

John was happy for his daughter. He had enjoyed

seeing her grow from a bubbly toddler, to become a delightful and beautiful young woman. Like all fathers he had wondered who she would marry and was now content with her choice. Sean was a typical young immigrant. He was stable and a handsome, sun tanned, six feet tall man and was part owner of a successful farrier business. What more could a father want for his daughter?

Summer had been very hot with gusting north winds. They had expected rain for the last few weeks. Dark clouds kept forming in the west but no rain. The grass had browned and the river was low. John and Sean had driven the cart down to the river with cans and filled them with water to top up the house water tank – just in case.

The first sign of the bushfire was smoke from the north, way in the distance. The fire was far away but the wind was strong. The smoke slowly increased and was coming in their direction. The horses were of concern. He knew that if the smoke became much stronger, he would have to blindfold them to keep them from panicking. There was little else they could do, other than watch and wait. They had kept the immediate area around the house and stable clear of any flammable materials. Valuables, keepsakes and some clothes had been packed in the cart, in case they had to leave in a hurry.

Late in the afternoon the heat had become more oppressive and they could smell the smoke. They planned to go to town if the fire jumped the far river bank and the trees ignited. The sky was noticeably darker, the clouds still forming and the smoke contributed to the gloom.

The grass in the paddocks fortunately was low and had not grown for a few weeks due to the lack of rain.

The leasee had moved his sheep a week ago. The horses were being hand fed from bales of fodder stowed in the stable. John was hopeful the fire would not become a risk in the paddocks. The fire continued towards the river. They took turns sleeping and watching the fire approach. At night the skyline was a red glow with occasional bursts of flames leaping upwards. The entire northern countryside was illuminated for as far as the eye could see.

Around dawn the wind shifted to a westerly and the fire slowed and was now moving along the far river bank. More clouds were gathering and the sky was becoming darker. The first of the river gums exploded into flames quickly followed by others. Within minutes the opposite side of the river bank was burning. The flames leapt into the air, climbing the trees relentlessly and destroying all in its path.

Then slowly the fire died down with only smoke billowing into the air. The wind change had stopped the bushfire crossing the river – for now. It seemed to be burning itself out! The wind from the west was strong and turning the bushfire towards itself and stopping its progress.

John watched the smoke all day, wondering what was going to happen next. Overcome by lack of sleep, he dozed off in a chair on the veranda. Jane and Sarah had gone to bed. Just before dawn he awoke with a start. There was tinkling on the roof. Rain! Stepping out from under the eaves, he looked up to enjoy the rain drops on his face and called Jane and Sarah to join him. He turned to the river and even the smoke had gone. The rainfall was not heavy but it was constant and most welcome. By the second day the bushfires in the district had been extinguished. Rain continued to fall and was not stopping.

He realised he had been lucky. But what of his neighbours to the north? He told Jane he was riding to town to see how the bushfire had affected others and see how they could help.

The Mayor had nominated the Mechanics Institute Hall as a relief centre for any families affected by the bushfire. When John arrived he was inundated with queries regarding the fire damage in his area.

It appeared that the fire had claimed at least five homesteads and countless livestock but fortunately no one had perished. Several of the farmers who had lost farms were in the hall and were being comforted by friends. John had not been acquainted with these families.

The Mayor had already started to arrange an event to raise money to help them in their time of need, such as a dinner or dance. William asked John to be on the committee, to which he readily agreed. The committee eventually numbered twenty who would be ushers, cooks, table servers and any other task identified. William organised the band.

The committee agreed to hold the suggested dinner dance in the Mechanics Institute Hall and to ask the participants for donations. The meal would be prepared by volunteers and would have a nominal charge to go to the Fund. The event was advertised in shop windows and the local newspapers and invited all comers.

The evening duly arrived and the hall soon filled. After a few speeches, the dining commenced. Naturally being a country town, all the food had been donated – vegetables, fruit and various meats. The ushers, cooks and table servers excelled themselves. How were they judged? No one complained! After an hour most of the clinking of knives and forks ceased. The male volunteers went around the tables, soliciting donations.

The banks, churches, clubs and some private donors had already contributed to the fund. When counted, the princely sum of one hundred and ninety six pounds had been raised. William put the donations in a leather satchel and locked it under the stage.

The band consisted of a piano player, two fiddlers and an accordion player and started with a waltz which had most of the seniors dancing but when the Irish tunes were played the younger generation took over the floor performing energetic jigs or reels. The band was flexible and played requests to satisfy one and all.

Around nine o'clock some of the outlying farmers left for their distant properties. John and Jane joined them. Sarah was staying overnight with William's daughter Mary in town. Some of the town residents also left. Most of those who remained lived in town. The band was getting ready to leave. Most people were tired and were sitting down talking. All had enjoyed their meals, the dancing and the volunteers were delighted with the donations raised.

Suddenly the hall main doors burst open and in ran three armed and masked men. "Everyone move to the back wall. This is a robbery. We want the donation money and your valuables. If you hand them over no one will be hurt. First we will have your valuables and then the donation money." The three robbers were very nervous and kept looking left and right.

Sean was standing next to Sarah. She moved closer to him, slightly behind his shoulder. One robber was standing near the bar.

The other two had approached a drover next to Sarah. The tall robber pointed his revolver at him and said, "You first. Put your money in his hat." He pointed to the second robber who was standing alongside him.

He then moved to Sarah. "I'll have your locket." She handed it over. He then said, "I'll have a kiss, too" and moved towards her. A ferocious Sean sprang forward and grabbed the arm holding his pistol and punched him hard in the face, spinning him around. He charged him, shouldering him into the wall. The robber's head hit the wall with a resounding thud and he collapsed to the floor. Sean turned to the second robber who fired his revolver at him, the bullet hitting him in the upper left arm. Sean's fury had taken over common sense. He punched the second robber in the jaw. At same time the robber fired his revolver a second time and the bullet struck Sean above his left hip. He threw two more punches as the robber slumped groggily to the floor.

The third robber turned to see what was happening. A shearer grabbed two bottles from the bar and threw them at him. The first bottle hit his shoulder and as he turned, the shearer threw the second bottle. This bottle hit the robber in the face and smashed into pieces creating a shower of blood. As he raised his hands to his face he was tackled by two shearers. One bent his arm back and the other picked him up and threw him to the floor, breaking the arm holding his revolver with a sickening crack and a scream came from him.

The whole confrontation had only taken a few minutes. There was silence for a few seconds; only one woman was screaming.

Then someone yelled, "Get some straps."

Two men ran to their gigs and quickly returned with bridle straps. Within a few minutes the robbers were strapped, hand and foot, regardless of their injuries. Together with the unconscious man, they were carried to a store room and locked in and guarded until the police arrived. Within two days the robbers were heading to Melbourne and the ultimate sentence.

The people were standing around shocked at what had happened. William Miles showed why he had been elected Mayor. He went to the band and asked them to play a waltz. He went to his wife and they started to dance. Soon others joined them. Others still a little unnerved were sitting drinking tea or something stronger from the bar. The Mayor had managed to recover the evening and the funds were still safe under the stage ready for banking the following morning.

Sean was taken into a side room. One of the wives had some medical experience and offered to check his injuries. The first bullet had gone through the side of his upper arm muscle but had not touched the bone.

A tight bandage soon stopped the bleeding. Blood was all down the left side of his clothing. The second bullet that struck him above his hip was of concern. Blood covered his clothing in the area and looked serious. When they checked it, they were amazed to see that the bullet had not penetrated his body. It had stuck a sovereign in Sean's money belt. He had a deep red circular mark above his hip around which a bruise was starting to show. All the blood on his clothes was from the upper arm injury.

Sean's wounds soon healed and he was back busy as usual at the forge and shoeing horses. He still wore the belt with the sovereigns and didn't even repair the damage.

During a weekend visit to Woodlea, John asked Sean, if he would have reacted differently if he was faced with the same situation again.

Sean thought for a moment. "No, I had my revolver in my left riding boot but I wouldn't have used it. There were too many people in the room."

John said, "I didn't know you had a revolver."

Sean pointed to his saddle bag. "It's in there. It's become a habit to carry it. It has memories for me."

The Navy Colt .36 was wrapped in a cloth. John was impressed. He could see it was new and virtually unused. He asked if he had ever fired the gun.

Sean shook his head. "No. Why?"

John laughed. "Well, you would have had to fire the pistol twice. The first chamber has no percussion cap fitted. It's good a thing you didn't try. Let's see if the other chambers fire. Come outside."

John aimed down towards the river and pulled the trigger six times. There were only three explosions. He told Sean he would have it cleaned and reloaded at the barracks. Sean's revolver needed more care and attention to be effective.

John had a message from William Miles in his mail box. "Could we meet for lunch? We need to discuss something."

He walked to the Mayoral office and knocked on his glass door. William waved, picked up his coat and joined him in the Council Chambers foyer. They shook hands and walked down to the hotel dining room.

After sitting down, William said, "Don't be alarmed at what I have to say. Wait until I finish."

John immediately felt uncomfortable.

William continued. "John, I'm putting the bottom forty acres on the market. I need some cash for a business venture. It will not involve your cottage. I will be advertising from next week and I wanted to tell you before you saw the sign."

John relaxed. Several times he had wondered about how long they would be able to stay in the cottage. He knew sooner or later they would have to leave.

John nodded. "Thank you. I appreciate that business is what it is and I am mindful that our time to go must come eventual. When it does, can I have first option?"

William replied, "Yes, I give you my word." They then changed the subject and enjoyed their meal and went their separate ways.

When Sarah told Sean about the For Sale sign, he had a good look at the land. He had always held a secret wish to own a farm but hadn't followed it up. Now with marriage on the horizon, this could be the time.

The land was well grassed and fronted a small river. He had told Sarah, he and a friend once mined for gold at Heathcote but nothing more. He wondered what Sarah would say if he told her he could be interested in buying the property. She had once mentioned it would be nice to own a home one day.

His first thought was – how much would it cost? He had three hundred pounds plus interest in Melbourne, twenty sovereigns in his belt and a balance of twenty pounds in the Kyneton Bank of Australasia. He decided to have a confidential meeting with the Mayor.

Mid-morning Sean visited the Mayor to arrange a meeting with him. He was fortunate. He was free and was ushered into his office. "Welcome, Sean. Please have a seat. What can I do for you?"

"I could be interested in buying your property. Can you tell me what your price is?"

William thought before he answered. "I'm looking for a cash settlement. I have a time limit for a project." He paused, waiting for Sean's response.

"At the moment I only want to know the price and maybe I will talk with you again, and also I want our discussion kept confidential."

William answered, "One hundred and sixty pounds cash in thirty days."

Sean said, "Thank you. Can I see you again next week?"

William's secretary entered. He stood up and shook Sean's hand. "Sorry, I have another appointment. Until this time next week. Goodbye." William wondered where a young man like Sean would get that amount of money.

Sean had a dilemma. Should he buy the land alongside his father-in-law, or should he offer to buy the block his father in law lived on, or both? What would John think? He would prefer to buy both properties but he wasn't sure he had enough money to do so and he didn't want to borrow. Who should he talk with? He decided he would talk it over with William tomorrow. Perhaps he could suggest a solution.

That evening, while Sean was sitting in the bar, a thought suddenly entered his mind. What about their mine, El Dorado? Would it still have value now? That night he wrote to Ben c/- the Heathcote Cobb and Co. office.

Four days later, up rode Ben. Sean was delighted to see his friend again. The two friends walked to a park bench.

Ben spoke first. "I have been intending to write to you as I have some news you will be interested in."

"I didn't expect to hear from you for weeks."

Ben laughed. "I rarely go into Heathcote. I have a farmer friend and I spend some time helping on his farm. I enjoy the company and I need a change of scenery. I've also been busy digging and panning with only limited success. Incidentally, here's a cheque for five pounds. I found some gold and sold it for fifteen pounds. After my expenses, that's your share."

Sean shook his friend's hand, nodding his head in delight.

"That's enough about me. What's your life been like since you've been here?"

"Well, this business is successful and I will be a part owner by the end of the year." Sean continued. "I'm engaged to be married within a few months. That's the reason I wanted to meet with you. I want to buy a property and I need another fifty or so pounds. I was hoping the mine might have some value, but if you are still working it, it would be unfair for me to ask you to find another interested person."

Ben laughed. "Well, you're wrong. I have been thinking of going home to California for a while and I'm happy to sell it. At the moment the two mines alongside ours have new miners working them. They are drilling four inch holes and taking soil samples from those mines. They have asked to drill some holes on our mine at no cost to us. I agreed. The results from the other mines have been showing a possible reef. I'm here to get you to come back with me to talk with them. Perhaps we can negotiate a deal."

Sean nodded. He could get away for a few days, but he needed to talk with William first.

Sean gave Ben the key to his room and asked him to wait there for him. He then went to William's office. He had to wait for him to return from a morning meeting. Sean stood up when William approached. "Can I see you now? It's urgent."

William opened the office door and gestured Sean to be seated.

Sean asked immediately, "Mr Miles, how much do you want for both properties?"

William thought for a moment. "Sean, do you have money? I cannot wait for a bank mortgage arrangement."

"Yes, I have enough for one property and I may have enough for both but I need to know your price,"

William wrote –

The river property – 160 pounds.
The house property – 220 pounds
Both properties   – 370 pounds

Sean had 325 pounds not including the sovereigns.

He picked up the paper. "Can you wait a week? I think I will have the money by then."

William shook his hand and nodded. "One week and, as you wish, it will be confidential."

Sean went back to his room to meet with Ben and head to Heathcote, after making a quick detour to the Emporium to tell Sarah he would be away for a few days at the Heathcote mine.

The ride to the Heathcote mine was thirty-five miles and through difficult terrain. They arrived at the El Dorado early evening and after a bite to eat and tea, the two tired riders were soon asleep in their bed rolls. The night was cool and starry and had brought back memories to Sean.

Early next morning Sean was awoken by the 'putt-putt' of a steam engine.

Ben had cooked eggs and meat ready for breakfast. He pointed to the machine about twenty feet away driving a belt and a wheel with pipes through a gear box contraption.

This was the all-important soil sampling drill.

After the hearty meal, Ben and Sean walked over to a group of men. The obvious leader, Ian Smythe, smiled and welcomed Ben, who in turn introduced Sean as his partner.

The leader said, "Good to meet you. Can we sit and talk? We are interested in working your mine in our right, if we can come to an arrangement." He paused. "I have to leave for Melbourne today to report on this area and hopefully we can do so before I leave."

Ben nodded. "Yes, I feel sure we can. I notice that you are bringing up shale rock and a few small pieces of white ore. That's a good sign."

Ian Smythe replied, "I can see you know mining. As you also know, until we dig, we are gambling. By taking samples we reduce the odds of failure. I'm gambling now but I'm prepared to offer you eighty pounds to take over working your mine."

Sean was delighted but Ben immediately said, "No, one hundred and twenty pounds is our price."

Ian Symthe's answering offer was: "One hundred pounds and that's my last offer. Take it or leave it."

Sean held his breath.

After the longest minute ever, Ben finally said, "Yes, agreed."

The three shook hands; the deal was done.

Sean's legs were shaking. He had to sit down.

Ian Smythe wrote out two fifty pound cheques for them, there and then.

Sean now had the capital he needed. His assets were now three hundred and seventy five pounds; just enough.

What would he tell John? Would he be comfortable with his son-in-law being his landlord?

Ben and he headed back to Kyneton and Ben joined Sean in a room at the hotel.

Sean did not wait until the following week. He went to see William the next day.

William saw him coming and opened the door.

Sean came straight to the point. "Mr Miles, I have the money for both properties."

"Sean, after you left, I remembered that I promised John to give him first option to purchase the house property. I'm embarrassed; I just forgot. Can you discuss your interest in the purchase with him? It might help solve my problem. After all, nothing will physically change for John and Jane."

Sean changed the subject. "I have the money you asked but I'm only prepared to pay three hundred fifty pounds in cash. If I pay your price I will be broke and I do not wish to be penniless when I marry. Let's decide a price and then talk about your promise to John."

"I'll think about it tonight. Drop by first thing tomorrow morning."

Sean nodded. He needed to think tonight as well.

John had lost interest in the sale of the lower paddock. Sean could not think of a way to broach the subject to tell him he was negotiating to buy both properties. Perhaps the direct approach was the only way.

He discussed his dilemma with Ben who agreed the direct approach was best. Why not? Get it over quick! It was also a way for John to release William from his promise. Yes, he would see John tomorrow.

Sean walked to John's office and entered.

John looked up. "Hello. To what do I owe this pleasure?" He could see Sean was uncomfortable.

"John, I hope you don't mind but I want to buy both of Mr Miles properties but I believe you have first option." He stopped talking.

John looked at him in amazement. "Do you have that sort of money?"

Sean nodded. "Yes, I owned a profitable gold mine and now that I'm marrying I want to build a home for Sarah and I like the area where the properties are.

Nothing will change; you and Jane will continue as now. I'll build a separate home for Sarah and myself. Mr Miles said you have first option on the home property." He waited for John to reply.

John sat there thinking for a minutes. "Well firstly, I'm delighted that you are buying a property for the both of you. Secondly, I have some money put aside and perhaps rather than build a new house, I can put it into extending the current building to suit all of us. The house is in the prime position. Thirdly, I'll speak with William about the option."

Sean heaved a sigh of relief. He had been worrying for nothing.

When he left, John poured a tea, closed his office door and sat there, hardly believing what he had just heard. Sarah had said nothing. Had Sean told her yet?

No, Sean had yet to tell Sarah of his negotiations for the properties. He wanted to be sure he had the purchase arranged first and not give her false hopes. He walked to the Emporium and asked Sarah to come to see him before she went home.

Her shop was going well. She now worked four days a week and her customer base was increasing weekly.

Sean left the workshop early and was waiting outside for her. He kissed her and arm in arm they walked to the hotel dining room and ordered tea and scones. He sat opposite her and looked into her eyes. "I have a surprise for you. I've bought a property for us."

She laughingly asked, "Really, where is it? Is it close to work?"

"No, not really. It's out of town."

"Does it have a house?"

"Yes, but it needs to be extended." He teased her.

"Have I seen it?" She asked.

"You see it every day and you will see it tonight."

Sean decided not to tease her anymore. "I bought your two blocks."

Sarah looked at him. "Do you mean you own our home?"

He said "No, *we* not me, own your home and eighty acres."

Sarah started to cry. "That's wonderful. Wait until I tell Mum and Dad."

Sean said nothing; he was enjoying her happiness so much.

After Sarah headed home to tell her mother and father the good news, Sean met with Ben for dinner. He told of how the meeting with John went. He felt content. Tomorrow he would see William and finalise the price and paperwork.

William was unsure of Sean's comment regarding the price. Was he bluffing? Three hundred and fifty pounds was a reasonable price and he seemed determined. He decided to accept his offer and complete the transfer as soon as possible.

When Sean arrived he could sense that his offer was acceptable. He and William shook hands and the deal was done. He would travel to Melbourne and collect a bank cheque in the name of William Miles. There were three hundred and fourteen pounds in Melbourne. He withdrew three hundred pounds by cheque. The fifty pounds from the mine sale had been deposited. He requested that when the cheque was cleared, another bank cheque for fifty pounds be forwarded immediately to Mr Miles c/- the Kyneton Council Chambers.

When he returned to Kyneton, he visited William and gave him the main cheque and told him the other should arrive in a week or so. The property transfers were not urgent and could wait until the second cheque arrived.

CHAPTER TWELVE

The Wedding

Regardless of the good news concerning the properties, the wedding plans continued. Jane and Sarah were busy compiling a guest list, arranging the catering and the church service. Mrs Jones was making the wedding dress with input from the women, although she would have preferred to design it herself.

As neither Sarah nor Sean had relatives in Victoria, the guest list comprised the friends they had made, including some of John's police friends, but they still numbered sixty. The church was large for only sixty people, but in a country town others would come to the wedding as observers. Any event helped ease the boredom of a country weekend afternoon.

The four of them were now well known in the district. Most locals knew John as a policeman and Jane as his strong willed wife. Sean was known to the horse owners and Sarah through her Emporium dress shop.

Jane had arranged for the catering to be carried out by the Royal Hotel and for the reception to be held at the Mechanics Institute Hall. The final fitting of Sarah's dress had been completed to the women's satisfaction.

John was looking forward to the big day and had written a brief speech which Jane insisted on vetting, although he said, "I'm not changing a word regardless of your opinion." Jane read it and handed it back to him without comment. He never found out if she agreed with the wording.

Sarah had William's daughter, Mary, as her bridesmaid and Sean had asked Ben to stay and be his best man. Ben agreed, although he was eager to go home, now that he had made up his mind to leave Victoria.

Sarah had arranged their suits through the owner of the men's wear shop in the Emporium. All they had to do was to be measured and then fitted. All was well.

A week before the wedding, the Inspector walked into John's office. "You won't like this, but Melbourne wants you there tomorrow. I've booked you on the nine o'clock Cobb & Co. stage. I don't know why. You are to travel in plain clothes and you will be met by Inspector Alford. He will brief you. Keep me posted and good luck."

John was angry, even though he knew the wedding was all arranged, he wanted to stay in Kyneton this week.

Jane just said, "Make sure you're home by Friday night."

John was still angry when he stepped off the coach.

Inspector Alford could sense he was not happy. "John, you will be home for the wedding, I guarantee it; I'm a guest." He hailed a cab and they headed to Collingwood and stopped outside a small two bedroom dwelling. "This is your home and office while you are in Melbourne. Your team is already here."

When they entered, newly promoted Acting Sergeants Evans and Stirling stood up and shook his hand. "Welcome back, sir."

John smiled. "Well, maybe. I don't know why I'm here yet."

The Inspector gestured. "Please be seated. I regret to say we have identified possible corruption within our ranks in Melbourne and you have been assigned by me to investigate. We will debrief here on Friday morning's."

He continued. "You have the rest of the week to plan your strategy. In this box is the information I have gathered so far. The first problem is – we are having evidence files vanish from the barracks' north block.

"The second problem is – how did two prisoners escape from custody at the Pentridge Stockade? One was your acquaintance Darcy Sykes. John, you will live here, the other room will be your operations room. Under no circumstances are any of you to visit the Melbourne Barracks. As I said, I'll visit you each week. Good bye for now." He turned and quickly left the building.

John knew he had a good team. He remembered their efforts with his previous task force. They sat down, opened the box and withdrew the briefing documents giving details of the escapes and listing the evidence files that had vanished. The blackboard was soon filled with dates. They then started to list personal names mentioned, looking for a pattern. John soon realised he needed a system to isolate or identify respective personnel. He would start on that tomorrow.

John asked Inspector Alford for a list of all administrative officers and the police personnel rosters for the north block staff over the last twelve months as well as a copy of the procedures detailing the handling of evidence files.

Immediately he identified that the procedures allowed for some slack tracking of files and the subsequent deliberate misplacement or otherwise. He would write up an improved procedure at the end of the investigation.

The team sat down to select specific groups of persons to exclude. The first eliminated were junior constables, followed by most of the administrative staff and then the cadets. This left a list of twenty personnel who handled, or who had access to, the files. Cross checking rosters, dates of the thefts and police names mentioned in the handling of the files, showed seven names of interest – four sergeants and three constables. The board also revealed one particular legal firm was involved in most of the missing files. John wanted the seven policemen's financial situations examined.

When Inspector Alford arrived on Friday morning John briefed him on their progress and asked him to authorise his team to carry out financial checks next week, after they returned from the wedding.

John and Inspector Alford left for Kyneton by coach mid-morning. The coach horses either galloped or cantered, depending on the steepness or otherwise of the road and covered around ten miles per hour. It was an American coach and the ride was fast and smooth with their leather strap suspension.

The English coaches had metal springs and gave a rougher ride and subsequently they had to travel slower. Their coach dropped off or picked up passengers at Keilor Fields, Sunbury Gap, Gisborne, then up through the dreaded thirteen mile trip to Woodend.

Arriving finally in Kyneton early evening they were met by Sean and Ben, who escorted the Inspector to his room at the Royal Hotel while John went to the barracks, saddled his horse and rode home to Woodlea to be greeted by a relieved wife and daughter, nervously looking forward to the wedding. They had an early night but the excitement of the pending big day made sleep difficult.

Jane had written out a list of things to do and was happy all of the tasks had been completed, particularly the fitting and delivery of the dresses and suits.

Sean and Ben rose early and went for a walk around town. The day was sunny, cool and with a gentle breeze, perfect for a wedding. They had an early lunch, then dressed and leisurely strolled the two blocks to the church.

At Woodlea, the feeling was not so relaxed. The hairdresser was late and caused Jane a mild panic. She was more flustered than Sarah who kept telling her, "Just sit down and relax. We have plenty of time."

As soon as William Miles delivered Mary, Jane became fully occupied with the task of helping the two girls dress in their gowns.

John sat quietly watching the proceedings, smiling to himself as he enjoyed their behaviour.

With an hour to spare, they were ready to go to the church. Jane and Mary went in the first gig, ten minutes before John and Sarah, who would arrive at the church on the hour in the second gig.

Sarah's dress was bulky and John needed to help her into the gig. They trotted out onto the road to town, talking about everything and nothing – passing the time! Both were a little nervous. It was an exciting day.

On the outskirt of town a kangaroo suddenly bounded across the road in front of Clare. She shied and galloped a few paces off the road into a ditch. John heard the wheel crack and felt the gig tilt. He stepped out and saw that one wheel had two spokes snapped. He helped Sarah step down. He could see that the gig was unable to be driven any further. His priority was to get Sarah to the church.

Saturday was a quiet day and few people would be travelling on this road.

He unharnessed the horse and tried to help Sarah to sit on the horse and ride to town by herself, but due to the design of her wedding dress, she kept slipping off. They decided to walk and hoped help would soon come by.

When they had not arrived on the hour and were five minutes late, Sean knew something was wrong, John would not be late without a good reason. He asked Ben to borrow a horse and ride out see what had happened. Within five minutes Ben found them walking to town. Without asking what had happened, he said to Sarah, "Take my horse and get someone to send a gig for us. Go quickly."

With stirrups, Sarah was able to stay in the saddle and cantered away.

John told him what had happened as they walked towards town. Ten minutes later help arrived and they were driven to the church with Clare tied behind.

The service was half an hour late as Sarah needed a bit of attention after the horse ride in her wedding dress. So be it.

The church was over half full and as expected many non-guests had assembled, just to enjoy another's wedding day on a pleasant country Saturday afternoon and admire the bride.

The service went smoothly. As expected Jane cried while John just kept smiling. Leaving the church seemed to take forever. Everyone wanted to shake hands with the groom or kiss the bride. Some people had never met them before and probably would never again.

After the wedding, Sean and Sarah were driven to the reception at the Mechanics Institute Hall, in a Hansom cab.

Jane and John drove their other gig with Clare still tied behind.

The hall was typical of most country towns. They were used by the community for meetings, weddings, wakes, elections, libraries, festivals and markets, to name a few. Many were made of bluestone, some red brick and in the very small towns, even weatherboard. But nearly every settlement had a community hall. This hall was bluestone outside with white painted plastered inside walls.

Paintings of civic leaders, mayors and presidents of associations stared down at the mere mortals who visited the hall. Association Honour Boards were also on display for all to see. Each hall had its own character.

The normal speeches were delivered. Jane had instructed the speakers not to be too verbose, to keep their speeches brief and to the point. She told John as well. She had been to other weddings where long and rambling speeches had almost ruined a reception. It was not going to happen today.

Ben kept his short. Sean's reply was even shorter and John's was warmly applauded. He smiled at Jane.

The meal was as expected in a country town, plentiful with fresh vegetables, fruit, various meats and was very filling. The fiddles, accordions and piano soon had the adults in a dancing mood. Sarah and Sean did a circuit of the hall first and signalled the others to join in. Jane had been teaching Sean for four weeks before he felt comfortable to do the bridal waltz. The newlyweds quietly left the hall and went back to Sean's hotel to change and then catch the last Cobb and Co. stage coach to Melbourne. It had been a long day.

John escorted Inspector Alford to the coach.

He thanked John for the wedding invitation. "I thoroughly enjoyed myself, especially the Scottish reels. They reminded me of my childhood days in Aberdeen. Good bye for now. I will see you during the week." A quick wave and the coach headed to Melbourne.

John took Jane's gig out the next day to replace the broken wheel. He had a spare wheel the same size that fitted both gigs. The broken wheel could wait until Sean and Sarah returned from Melbourne.

CHAPTER THIRTEEN

Mystery Solved

A kiss from Jane and he was off to Melbourne again.

Monday morning, the team sat down to further separate the people of interest. After two days they had reduced the names to four that reoccurred several times – an articled clerk, two sergeants and a constable. Inspector Alford said he would handle the clerk.

The clerk worked for the Crown Prosecutors office and had the responsibility of distributing evidence files between the police records office and his C.P. office lawyers. The Inspector said he could keep John's investigation secret if it appeared a senior police officer had discovered the clerk had mishandled a particular file.

John's team now investigated each suspect's financial status. The two sergeants had bank accounts with deposits in excess of their salaries.

The first sergeant was interviewed and broke down in tears, admitting to having been paid to destroy files. He was immediately suspended and charged. He was due to retire within the month and would probably lose his pension.

The second sergeant denied the allegation and refused to say where he had obtained the extra money in his bank account. There was no direct evidence to be able to charge him. However, he resigned on the spot and left Victoria.

The constable was a surprise, his bank account was reasonable. When John checked his file, he found that he had been a sergeant and had been demoted for neglect of duty several years ago.

The team quietly followed him for two weeks. The Saturday of the second week, the constable rode out of Melbourne to a farm at Tullamarine. On Monday John checked with the records office and found he owned the farm.

The constable was unable to explain where he obtained the money to purchase the farm and was arrested and charged. Eventually he admitted his role in deliberately losing evidence files.

During these two weeks, John had been writing a procedure for handling evidence files. The new requirements required that all completed police evidence files be deposited in a secure records room. A file would only be released by the presentation of a letter of authority from the duty inspector. The receiving constable must sign a register and complete the tracking details required – who for, where to, when and why. A sergeant would hold the key and only he and the records clerk were permitted to enter the records room. After delivery of the files, the constable would receive a receipt from the Crown Prosecutor's office and return the receipt to the police records sergeant. This process completed a cyclic tracking record of files and the persons who had handled them.

Inspector Alford arrived Friday to update them on the progress from his investigation. He started first by saying the articled clerk had been sacked. Doubt still existed about his actions and who else could have been involved. He then detailed the charges relating to the other offenders.

John spoke of the results he and his team had uncovered. Basically the police force was at fault due to their poor management of the documents. They were being handled without any thought of their security, level of importance and staff accountability.

Rather than dwell on the past discrepancies, John presented his suggested improved procedures draft to the Inspector for his consideration and action as necessary.

The meeting closed with the Inspector thanking them for their contribution, of not only identifying the offenders but also for proposing a realistic and common sense procedure. He had realised earlier that the problems were due to lack of supervision and poor record keeping standards.

Locating the prime offenders and implementing tight procedures should prevent files from vanishing or being misplaced. A report on the investigation was circulated within the barracks.

As an afterthought, the Inspector mentioned that Darcy Sykes had been rearrested at the docks. During his arrest he had killed an associate. His sorrowful career would be ended with his hanging. Regarding the prisoner escapees, the authorities at the Pentridge Stockade had located two warders who had been paid to open a side gate in the dark hours. They were now prisoners themselves.

John's team was no longer required and was reassigned. Inspector Alford saw him to his stage coach and mentioned that Inspector Brittan was to be promoted and would be returning to Melbourne and John would become the Acting District Inspector. A quick wave and John headed home.

CHAPTER FOURTEEN

Promotions All Round

A civic farewell was held for Inspector Brittan's departure with at least half the town attending. He was presented with a scroll from the council for his contribution to the community. A two week handover went smoothly, allowing John to settle into his new role. At least he would no longer be called on to perform short term duties in Melbourne. He was now domiciled in Kyneton.

The barracks door burst open. A breathless man entered and yelled. "There's trouble at the Cobb and Co. office. Your constables need help." John quickly collected his pistol and ran to the roadway following two other constables. Their office was only four buildings away. He could see a crowd had gathered.

Constable Moore saw John approaching and ran to him. "Two men tried to rob the mail bag from the office but the driver refused to hand it over and was shot. I don't know if it is serious. I have a constable around the back at the stables watching the horses. They're trapped but two employees are still inside. I waited for you."

John nodded. "Send another constable to the back and come with me."

A stage coach was tied to a post outside the office. John said it needed to be moved.

Sean had arrived and heard John's comment to Constable Moore. "I'll do it." Before John could stop him he was running to the hitching post. After a quick knife cut severing the halter, he led the coach away from the front of the office.

The robbers now had no means of escape. A loud voice bellowed, "I want to speak to the police. We'll surrender."

John answered, "Throw your guns out and I'll come in." Two pistols were hurled out a window onto the street.

John entered the office to be confronted by an angry giant of a man. "I hate you bastards. I know I will go to gaol for robbery, so I might as well go for assault as well."

He advanced on John and threw a wild swinging punch. John's experience from his boxing days ensured that he ducked under the punch and quickly punched the giant hard to the midriff. The giant sucked in some air and swung again and was hit in the midriff as before. With the wind knocked out of him, he charged.

John stepped back and struck him hard to the jaw. John immediately felt an excruciating pain in his left hand and lower arm, but instinct made him punch the giant with his right hand to the jaw. The giant collapsed unconscious to the floor.

A crowd had entered the office to watch the fight and clapped when the giant hit the floor. One person was heard to say, "He's as tough as his missus." The other robber stood in the corner with his arms raised and was arrested.

With the drama over John went to the doctor, who 'tut tutted' about today's violence. After a good look at the hand he placed both of John's hands on a table. He gave John a piece of soft wood to bite on and then started to pull his fingers straight and then push the hand bones roughly back into position.

John nearly bit through the wooden mouthpiece. The doctor placed his hand on a small panel the same size as his hand and then shaped a sea sponge to fit into the hollow of the inside of his hand. He then strapped the hand, the board and the sponge together. Several bones in his hand were broken but his forearm was intact. After six weeks the bandages were removed and, except for a small lump, his hand was almost fully functional. At least he could hold reins.

Inspector Brittan's promotion was now gazetted, as was John's. He was now the Kyneton District Police Inspector. Constable Moore had also been promoted, to sergeant. Inspector Brittan and Inspector Williams were required to attend an official function in Melbourne for their promotions to be acknowledged by their peers. Their wives were also invited, which delighted them both and gave them a chance to dress up. An excellent meal, short speeches and the presentation of certificates was enjoyed by all.

John had one unpleasant duty to attend to before he returned home. Jane had already gone home. He had been advised, while he was in Melbourne, he was required to witness two hangings – Darcy Sykes and a young man. As a newly promoted Inspector he could hardly protest. A senior police office was required to be a witness at all hangings. The hangings were to be at the Melbourne Gaol, an imposing and yet forbidding bluestone building across from the barracks.

The weather was cloudy with patches of rain. It

was in keeping with John's mood. He was not looking forward to the hangings. The constable at the gate checked his credentials and pointed him to the entry of the gallows building.

Six persons were already in the gallery, two newspaper reporters, a lawyer, a minister, a councillor, the warder and now John. He nodded to the silent group.

The masked hangman was standing on the scaffold. The door creaked and in came Darcy Sykes between to warders. He was quiet and walked slowly, his legs shackled and hands cuffed. As the minister approached him, he tripped on the steps. Darcy turned. "Are these steps safe? Be careful you don't hurt yourself. Someone might need you." They were his last words. He stepped onto the trapdoor. His head was covered, the bolt pulled, the trapdoor opened and it was all over in a matter of seconds.

John looked away.

The second hanging was just as quick, with the young man's last words: "I was to be married next month. Now I'll never know."

John was shaken by the experience and left the gaol as soon as he had signed the documents as a witness. He had no interest in socialising with anyone and left the gaol and Melbourne on the first coach next morning, looking forward to being home with his family.

CHAPTER FIFTEEN

A Murder

Kyneton was quiet and conservative, a typical country town. When a murder occurred it shocked the entire district. Events like that just didn't happen there!

It was Edward Sims, the man who had befriended John in Woodend on his way to Kyneton. He had been found dead by his wife in his stable. Sergeant Moore found her lying over the body, crying hysterically. There was a strong smell of alcohol. Mr Sims had been stabbed savagely three times in the back. The knife blade had snapped; a section of the blade was still in his back. The remainder of the kitchen knife was found in the straw on the stable floor.

Sergeant Moore had roped the area off and stationed a constable at the scene. A second inspection of the stable revealed a half empty bottle of whisky. He left the knife and bottle in the stable, covered over with saddle blankets.

As a serious crime had been committed, John was required to immediately notify Melbourne for a detective's presence. Meanwhile Sergeant Moore had gone into the house looking for anything he might consider unusual. The knife drawer did not have any implements with similar handles to the murder weapon. Finding nothing out of place, he returned to update John.

They walked back to the crime scene for John's briefing and to meet Mrs Sims. Surprisingly, she could not be found and a horse was missing. A young constable was assigned to question the neighbours to find out if the Sims' had any relatives in the Kyneton District. After an hour he came back without any information. Meanwhile a young lady had approached Sergeant Moore and asked if the police had notified Mrs Sims' brother who lived in Woodend. John remembered. "I have met him but I don't know his address."

Sergeant Moore advised John. He and a constable would go to Woodend and see if the local constable knew his address. Her absence under the circumstance looked suspicious.

John nodded and walked back to his office. He wondered if Edward could have been drunk, an argument ensued and got out of hand? But whom with?

John decided to visit the morgue to see if there were other wounds to Sims' body and to see if he had been drinking or not. He had the morgue attendant confirm his findings. He wrote a report and placed it in Sergeant Moore's incident file.

The Woodend constable had met Mrs Sims previously and took her to her brother's home. She was sitting outside with a man, when she saw the Kyneton policemen walking up the pathway. She started crying again.

After the customary cup of tea, Mrs Sims settled down and agreed to return to Kyneton. The three rode back, mainly in silence. The incident was not discussed. They wanted to carry out a formal interview, following the laid down procedures.

During the tea time, the sergeant noticed Mrs Sims smelt of alcohol. He was surprised and thought it unusual for a woman.

The interview was planned for the next morning. Mrs Sims was early and seemed relaxed. They agreed the interview would be informal. The detective had not arrived yet.

They initially asked her to relate what she had done on that day, from first thing in the morning up to finding her husband in the stable.

She was calm and spoke logically. When she finished, they decided to have a break. They didn't want to proceed too far without the detective. Fortunately he walked in just as they paused.

Detective Walsh appeared easy going and laid back. His first words were: "I hope I don't have to ride the stage coach very often over that corduroy road to Woodend. It was like riding over cobblestones at high speed." He hummed an Irish tune as he read the incident file and nodded to himself.

When the formal interview started John could see he knew his job. Mrs Sims repeated her story and immediately after the detective asked, "How much alcohol did you see your husband drink on the day he was murdered?"

Mrs Sims seemed startled and stuttered, "Yes, I saw him drink from a whisky bottle several times."

He continued. "Do you drink alcohol?"

She hesitated. "Well, yes, I do a little."

The next question was: "What would you say if I said I believe that your husband had not had an alcoholic drink on the day he was murdered but you had drunk half a bottle of whisky." She went white and stopped talking. Detective Walsh added, "We will leave you to have a think by yourself."

The Constable and the Miner

They then left the room.

Detective Walsh pondered. "Sergeant, the evidence statement from the morgue will be difficult for her to dispute. But have you identified a motive? You say in your report he was an ordinary person, good worker, community member and well liked. His wife has a similar report. However, I note the finding of several whisky bottles in the rubbish. What did the next door neighbours hear? Were there any confrontations? We need to find a motive."

Sergeant Moore looked for the written report from the constable who had been asked to do the neighbours' door knock. It wasn't in the file.

Moore went to look for him.

"It's in your mail box." The constable was young and hadn't realised it should have been placed in the incident file or handed directly to the officer in charge of an investigation. The report contained what they were looking for – a motive for the murder.

Mrs Sims had a vicious temper and often assaulted her husband. The next door neighbours often heard her screaming at him.

Sergeant Moore went to the local alcohol supplier and found out she was well known as a good customer. He knew of her husband but had not met him. So much for her story!

When they re-entered the interview room, Mrs Sims was a different woman. She was red faced, angry and started shouting. "You don't know what I had to put up with. Headaches day in, day out. Edward didn't care. Nobody did. Except my brother. He would listen. The whisky helped my headaches."

The detective asked her directly, "Why did you kill your husband?"

"We were arguing in the kitchen but he wouldn't listen to me.

"He told me I didn't need to drink and to get help. He didn't care. He turned his back on me and walked out to the stable, so I took a knife, followed him and stabbed him in the back." She stopped talking and began crying, holding her head in her hands.

The detective sent a constable to Woodend to bring her brother to Kyneton to discuss his sister's health issue. Her brother confirmed that she had suffered from headaches for many years and they appeared to be getting worse. With their evidence, this information and her confession, the investigation was virtually finished. Mrs Sims was charged with murder, arrested and taken to Melbourne for trial. However, a week prior to her trial, Mrs Sims collapsed in her cell, after suffering bleeding on the brain and died. This brought an end to the sorry saga. The town eventually returned to normal and the murder became a distant memory.

Several weeks after Edward Sims burial, his brother walked into John's office. "I have been unable to find my brother's money. Two months ago he showed me a roll of notes. I have searched his house from top to bottom without luck. I'm sure he still had the money when he was murdered. It might sound strange but could the money have been in his clothes he was buried in? I don't think they were changed."

John and Mr Sims went to the funeral parlour and they confirmed Edward Sims was buried in the clothes he was wearing when he was murdered. The brother's request to open the grave was granted and his idea was right. Sewn inside the wide waistband they found an envelope containing fifty pounds.

The next few months passed quickly. John's new role as the District Inspector propelled him into the community social scene. Initially he and Jane enjoyed meeting and making new friends. However, after a month or so, they began to find excuses to miss the more mundane events and only go to ones they preferred. The police work was routine with only a few drunk, assault and shop lifting offences. John still had reports to complete but he always felt he was waiting for his next challenge. He had a good team and was confident they would be able to handle whatever came their way.

At Woodlea, the building extension had occupied John and Sean's weekends. Three more rooms had been added to the current building, a large living-dining room and two smaller rooms, one a bedroom, the other a general purpose room for reading, a library and sewing.

During those months, three stonemasons had built the bluestone walls similar to the existing cottage walls. Carpenters had fitted floor and ceiling boards, windows and doors. John and Sean whitewashed the inside of the stone walls, window sills, doors, and had fitted locks. Jane had extended her garden outside the new rooms.

When it was completed, John and Jane walked down to the river to look back up at their home. It looked magnificent with the cloudless sky in the background. It was their 'Castle in the Sky'.

To celebrate the completion of the building extensions, Jane decided to have a family luncheon. Sean met George and Bridget at Cobb and Co. and drove them to Woodlea. John noticed that George carried his leather boxing bag. It was Bridget's first journey outside Melbourne and she was enjoying it immensely.

Jane had become a minor farmer. She had the three horses, a cow, three pigs, some chooks and the two dogs. Sean had purchased thirty ewes and a ram. He told her they were hers as she was more interested in them than he was.

Jane gave George and Bridget a complete tour of the farm, from the river, through the orchard, vegetable plot to the pig's pen and finally the stables. At the end of the stable they had made a small wooden shed for a milk separator. It was laborious cranking the handle to make butter from the cream but the results were well worth the effort. She even made tallow candles with cotton wicks from the boiled sheep's fat poured into wooden moulds and left to harden. Sperm oil in the lanterns gave better light but the candles were cheaper.

During lunch they chatted about everything and nothing. George and Bridget were the main contributors with news about Melbourne and from London and Melbourne newspapers they had read.

They brought some with them. After lunch they carried their drinks and sat outside on the veranda, looking down to the river. The sun was shining through the fruit trees casting shadows onto the multi-coloured garden. Sheep were sheltering under the river gum trees. It was a picture book scene.

George asked, "Dad, did you ever expect to be in a place like this when you left London?" They all looked at John.

He thought for a moment before he answered. "No, but I lived in the hope of a new and fulfilling life for us all. Now when I look at you all, with Sean a member of our family and maybe Bridget one day, I see contentment on your faces. We have each been happy and indeed lucky with our good fortune."

He stood up. "Jane loves the farm, Sarah's happy with her boutique, George's content in the hotel, Sean is successful with his current business and the El Dorado mine, and regarding me," he paused, "who would have considered that within five years I would be a Colony of Victoria District Police Inspector?"

Jane replied quietly. "Yes, we should thank God for our good fortune."

George said nothing; he just nodded in agreement. His father's decision to leave England had been a good one.

They sat on the veranda quietly talking, appreciating John's words and looking at the river water placidly flowing by.

DEFINITIONS

Bailed up   Held up by armed robbers generally on horse back.

Billabong   Land locked lagoon, left after receding river water.

Bosun (bo's'n) Boatswain, senior sailor below officer rank.

Carbine   Short rifle used by Mounted Policemen or Troopers.

Carlsruhe   Site of original Kyneton Gaol, Victoria.

Cartwright   Wagon or cart builder.

Cheesed   Lines (ropes) laid flat and coiled on deck.

Corduroy	Road surface made of poles or planks lain sideways.
Cronk (Aust)	Unsound, fraudulent.
Currency people	Born in the Colonies.
Damper (Aust)	Bread substitute. Kneaded flour with water and salt. Cooked in ashes. It was dense and heavy.
Dunny (Aust)	Small shed used for outside toilet over a hole in the ground. It would be moved to a new location as required.
Emigrant	Person leaving a country to stay in another.
Furling	Folding or gathering a sail closely.
Halyards	Ropes/lines to raise/lower sails.
Immigrant	Person arriving from another country to stay.
Hansome Cab	Two wheel horse drawn vehicle (taxi). Driver sat outside.
Joes	Name given to licence inspecting policemen. Name of the Governor of Victoria, Joseph La Trobe.
Larrikin (Aust.)	Urban hooligan.
Maluka	Boss (Aborigine name).

Mine	Claim size for two miners = 288 sq ft.
Missus (Aust.)	Wife.
McIvor	Original name for Heathcote, Victoria.
Mob (Aust.)	Large herd or flock of livestock/kangaroos.
Newgate prison	Main London prison. Many convicts left from there for the Colonies.
Offsider (Aust.)	Assistant to a manual worker.
Old Bailey Court	Main London court.
Peelers	Sir Robert Peel established the first genuine police force in the world when he formed the London body in 1829. Prior to then, London had the 'Bow Street Runners' endeavouring to keep law and order.
Penny (pence)	One twelfth of a shilling – pence is plural of penny.
Remittance man	Australian immigrant paid to stay away from UK. Banished.
Rattle	A wooden frame rotated by a handle causing a rattling sound when the tongue contacted a sprocket. Replaced by a whistle in 1884. It was heard over longer distances.

Ratlines	Rope ladder used by sailors to climb to sail/mast riggings.
Reefing	Reduce the surface area of a sail by tying straps together.
Rouseabout	Unskilled country/farm worker. General hand.
Shilling	Twelve pennies – twenty shillings equalled one pound sterling.
Shrouds	Ropes or lines supporting the mast and tied to the ship's side.
Slip rails	Three horizontal poles fitted loosely into holes in verticalpoles imbedded in the ground. Temporary paddock gate.
Smithy	Blacksmith.
Sterling people	Born in United Kingdom.
Sundowner (Aust)	Itinerant worker who visited farms for meal/bed at sunset.
Swag	Shoulder pack of folded bedding and possessions of itinerant wanderer or swagman.
The Gap	Location adjacent the town of Sunbury, Victoria.
Trooper	Mounted constable or soldier.

Van Diemen's Land	Original name for Tasmania.
Watch	A four hour duty spell on board a ship. (Except 'Dog watch' 1600 – 2000 hrs – which was split into two hourly spells.)
Way	Lost way – ship stopping. Under way – ship moving.
Yardarm	Horizontal cross beam, tied to a mast, from which a sail is slung.

NOTES

1850's - TRAVELLING TIMES

Approximately

SAILING SHIP

Liverpool/Cape Town – 75 days + Cape Town/Sydney – 40 days. (4 months.)

Sailing ships were required to travel on oblique angles. Tacking to obtain the best speed but subject to the weather and direction of the prevailing winds. Voyages took between four to six months.

STAGE COACH

COBB and Co. started in Victoria in 1853, during the gold rush period, and was an instant success. Generally the coaches had a team of either four or six horses, travelling at between eight and twelve miles per hour, galloping on flat roads and cantering up hills.

The fastest coaches changed their horse team around every ten miles. The slowest coach team was changed at roughly four hourly periods. Melbourne to Bendigo was a day trip. (120 miles in 12 to 15 hours.)

HORSE BACK

Generally a rider on a good horse could cover sixty miles in one day and up to one hundred miles in two days. It has been reported horses could cover up to a hundred miles in a day!

AUTHOR'S PROFILE

John P. F. Lynch

The Constable and the Miner is John's third historical novel. His first was *The Convict and The Soldier* followed by the sequel, *The Aborigine and the Drover*. The novels are set in the Australian Colonial period of the mid 1800's, viz. Tasmania and Victoria.

He has written several local history books and an autobiography.

His mother's great, great grandparents settled in the Kyneton district of Victoria, during the years of 1849-1855. John is a former member of both the Kyneton and Romsey Historical Societies, both of who helped him in his research for his books.

He travelled extensively during his 60 year career in aviation and has visited County Clare in Ireland and Cumbria in England to research his books.

John is a Member of the Order of Australia, a Knight Hospitaller of the Order of St John of Jerusalem and a Fellow of the Royal Victorian Association of Honorary Justices.

He is an ex-Australian Navy veteran, and was the President of the Romsey/Lancefield RSL for over nine years and is an **RSL Life Member.**

He is also a Life Member and a former President/Secretary of the Romsey Football/Netball Club.

A former Legatee of Macedon Ranges Legacy Group, John served a term as Chairman of the Group, Board Member of the Bendigo Club and long standing Sergeant of Arms.

His current community involvement is with the Craigieburn Memorial Remembrance Committee as Vice President.

BOOKS WRITTEN

By John P F Lynch

HISTORY/NOVELS

The Convict and the Soldier
The Aborigine and the Drover
The Constable and the Miner

HISTORY

St Mary's Church and Schools 1858 – 2006
The Romsey/Lancefield R.S.L. 75 YEARS
      1933 - 2008
The Romsey Football/Netball Club 1878 – 2009
Joseph Hall – Kyneton Pioneer 1804 – 1872.
A Lifetime's Journey – Autobiography

www.ingramcontent.com/pod-product-compliance
Lightning Source LLC
Chambersburg PA
CBHW070553010526
44118CB00012B/1306